Mini-Manual of The Independent Counterterrorist

Second Edition

R.J. GODLEWSKI

DEDICATION

To all, known and unknown, who dedicate their lives toward protecting the dignity and integrity of innocent human life.

.

CONTENTS

ACKNOWLEDGMENTS

To all who made the concept of *The Independent Counterterrorist* a success over the years, especially my beloved Sara (1951-2003) and Ms. Debbie Hamilton of Right Truth Blog.

1 WHY A 'TACTICAL CITIZEN'?

Have you ever seen a video or witnessed other people standing around and observing another individual being beaten, dying, or otherwise threatened without doing something about it? Do you know someone who goes catatonic as soon as adversity strikes? Have you ever met anyone who casts votes and yet remains clueless regarding politics, economics, and national security? Let us face it; the vast majority of the human population likely goes about his or her life with little thought beyond that which confronts their vision at that very moment. Such people live solely for that week's paycheck, drive automobiles while talking on cell phones, and entrust teachers with the rearing of their children. None of them considers "what if?" To make matters worse, scientists have proven that 65% of the human population can be induced into killing an innocent person with little more than "authoritative" prompting from another individual.[1] This means that *at least six of the next ten people that you encounter possess the inherent ability to kill* you with very little external motivation.

---

[1] Dave Grossman, *On Killing: The Psychological Cost of Learning to Kill in War and Society* (New York: Back Bay Books, 2009), 142.

The "'Me' Generation" has silenced rational thought in education, politics, economics, religion, and life in general. Big Brother has assured the world that the masses – specifically representing your friends and neighbors – defer to the state without a moment's reflection upon whether 'the state' represents your best interests or not. We can see this within America by how many people equate the "Occupy Wall Street" crowd with goodness and the various Tea Party participants with abject evil despite overwhelming evidence to the contrary. Remember, anarchy flourishes with crowds, not one or two individuals. More dangerously, perhaps, rests the existence of the United Nations (UN), an organization that does very little but equalize divergent countries. In fact, the UN could be considered, in modern socio-political terms, international affirmative action at best. Where the fault rests, unfortunately, is within any thought process that suggests that *actions* are equal.

Consider the UN in the light of domestic U.S. politics. Representative Nancy Pelosi (D-CA), over several years, reigned as Speaker of the House – the third in line to the U.S. Presidency. She was voted into office, however, by the district largely consisting of San Francisco, California. What this means, of course, is that the people of San Francisco placed into office a person whom the rest of the nation did not vote for or emphatically endorse. The UN represents the same problem; a myriad of smaller, largely insignificant nations could conspire to disrupt the planet over the objectives of those whose presence, experience, and talents have forged the opportunity for the UN to exist in the first place. This remains problematic, to say the least. At best, the UN indicts *all* organizations – both good and bad.

The concept of a 'tactical citizen', without whom there

could be no *independent* counterterrorists, rests upon the very foundation that it remains *individuals* who hold personal responsibility. That is, there are good *people* as well as *bad* people, but *people* they remain. Neither automatons nor animals. *Every* individual person conceived on this planet bears the same inherent rights as all other individuals, irrespective of his or her place in life, race, nationality, religious beliefs, education, or physical beauty. What separates people from one another, therefore, remains exclusive to his or her personal actions. The same holds true with groups of individuals, though responsibility for collective actions more often than not rests within the power of that particular group's leadership.

Because institutions – whether religions, organizations, governments, etc. – can be led astray by the actions of comparatively very few individuals (say, in the case of Nazi Germany), the holistic approach to significant activities may be dangerous. The larger the organization, the greater the opportunity for the few to destroy the reputation and livelihood of the many. For example, consider how the actions of a relatively few individuals who abused prisoners at Abu Ghraib, gang-raped a 14-year-old girl in Mahmudiyah, Iraq, or killed innocent Afghan citizens in Maywand destroyed the reputation of the U.S. military and Americans in general.[2] That so few could destroy so many has been the hallmark of humanity ever since Cain took Abel out into the field to murder him.[3] Hence, the desperate need for *independence* within the world and, more precisely, why *The Independent Counterterrorist* (ICT) represents neither an

---

[2] Clark C. Barrett, *Finding "The Right Way": Toward an Army Institutional Ethic* (Carlisle, PA: Strategic Studies Institute, September 2012), 2.
[3] The parable of Genesis 4:1-11 *New American Bible* remains that murder can arise from even the smallest (i.e., two) group. See the next chapter.

organization nor a doctrine.

This new edition of my book merges my *Tactical Citizen* and *The Independent Counterterrorist* programs[4] and rests as a strict matter of convenience. The attributes of one who seeks to protect his or her family from threat and disaster (TC) remains as valid as one who personally seeks to stop domestic and transnational threats (ICT) against the broader community. Accordingly, some will likely feel more comfortable protecting his or her home whereas the more ambitious will likely seek to stop harm against the innocent. Nevertheless both are sorely needed in today's day and age as hostile groups – from various political, social, and religious affiliations – seek to disrupt others' "life, liberty, and the pursuit of happiness."

It remains an old adage that one picture is worth a thousand words. Unfortunately, many people are taught by photographs more than learn from events or words. In this regard, you will find no photographs and a singular diagram within this book. It does not represent a training manual, per se. It is intended as a reference manual to inspire *you* – the budding Independent Counterterrorist – to learn on your own. The greatest disadvantage in the world of battle remains to permit your adversary to understand what it is that you know. Therefore, to succeed within life, *do not* allow your enemies to know exactly what it is that you have learned and can do. Plant this seed, water it, nourish it, and permit it to grow to new heights.

---

[4] Both programs emerged as a monthly, standalone training series with PDF documents posted on the Internet for ease and convenience. This book updates the previously release *Mini-Manual of The Independent Counterterrorist* and absorbs material from both efforts.

2 THE IMPERATIVE TO FIGHT.

Peace is the absence of the hostility; the aberration of the human condition. Wars, however, have been around ever since Cain took out his brother Abel in a fit of religious jealousy. Whether you subscribe this to a Biblical story of historical accuracy or not, the moral remains that as long as there are at least *two* people around, conflict naturally arises and it may result within personal death or injury. If such conflict arises with only one person around; well, then, we have to come and take that person away for safekeeping.

You might also note that this first of recorded conflicts was, in fact, a faith-induced struggle. The Lord looked upon Abel's offering with favor but not upon Cain and his. This pissed Cain off and the rest is history – people *are* different and their blessings will inspire others to rage. Today, in the 21st century, the same situation occurs, developed over decades by shoddy post-Colonial politics. The Middle East and Northern Africa (MENA) remains a prime example where Israel has risen from abject poverty to build a democratic nation of posterity and success while Arabs, particularly those within 'Palestine', descend into eternal poverty and envy of their Jewish neighbors. The Palestinians have simply descended into existence as perennial poster child of "the cause" and few care to extract themselves from the mess to forge a legitimate nation of his and her own. Blaming the West, and their avowed blood enemy Israel, appears easier to do than to fashion a respectable life of their own.

You would do well to begin a careful study of the rise of modern Israel with its conflicts among its neighbors, particularly its indefensible borders and significant 'illegal' immigration problem that represents something of a harbinger to difficulties associated with the United States' own national security. Israel's tactical problems today rest largely with this phantom nemesis of constantly shifting illegal immigrants.[5]

By the way, this is a good trait to nurture; to constantly read from within the historical narrative. Ours represents a world where the purveyors of mayhem remain a very well-read bunch.[6] It would be to your distinct disadvantage to assume that Islamic and narco terrorists remain any less literate. What you need to add to this – which our Western leaders have failed to grasp – is that history exists to learn from; it does not represent an abstract archive of secretive documents that escape our attention. You, as a budding counterterrorist 'agent', possess ten thousand years of predecessors from which to learn and emulate. Our wars, though relatively modern and technologically superior to, say, the Peloponnesian War, are nevertheless as barbaric and 'one-on-one' as that great three-decade struggle

---

[5] Benny Morris, *Israel's Border Wars: 1949-1956* (New York: Oxford University Press, 1997), 118-184

[6] Paul Balor, *Manual of the Mercenary Soldier* (Boulder: Paladin Press, 1988), 22-23.

between the Athenians and Spartans.

As I have thus written, first off and straight away, *peace* represents the rarity amongst our kind. People, for whatever ill-conceived and instantaneous justification, will descend into conflict long before charitable pursuits are even acknowledged. If this were not the case, then we would come flying together with open arms and wallets whenever a natural catastrophe occurs. You will note that even here within the compassionate United States, looting and even sometimes death occurs before the first telephone calls to relief agencies are made.

The *greatest* threat to your safety will come from that briefest hint of civility that descends upon you when the shit hits the fan. You will, I can almost guarantee, think "The authorities will restore order" or "I have lived here for decades and I have always managed to come through okay." There remains a first time for *everything*, do not forget. I have always characterized myself as "the most lethal individual that you will ever meet whose mannerisms and morality will betray his upbringing." In short, if I do not perceive you to be a threat to my existence, then neither do you need to perceive me to represent a threat to yours.

I have, on numerous occasions, defended myself against substantially larger opponents, sometimes even while in the presence of authorities. I have employed whatever tool or weapon that I could lay my hands upon, be it pencil, hammer, or swinging meat hook. Therefore, there is little that I will not improvise in order to defend myself should the need arise at work or at home. Naturally, others sometimes exclaimed, "Did you not understand that you could have been fired?" I usually responded with, "Did you *not* understand that I could have been killed unless I defended my life?"

My line between brutality and civility exists, but it remains extremely sharp. I could go from one limit to the other in a literal heartbeat and so too must you if you truly want to survive within this crazy, mixed-up world of ours. Will our efforts *always* work? Who really knows. All that we know for certain is that we were born kicking and screaming for a chance at life and we have made it thus far. I will not accept an unnatural death without doing *something* to assure longevity. The rest remains up to God's Divine Providence and Will.

You have to present this mentality of eternal survival too. To go through life within a "daze" is not very conducive to this survival. Neither is remaining timid, which is what a great deal of your neighbors prefer. Your terrorist enemies live for dying – rather, martyrdom – as long as they can kill as many of us Westerners as possible. Basically, it rests within their heritage, this Bedouin/Tribal form of Machiavellian reality. Some say do unto others before they do unto you. I say, that it remains all part of my fundamental rule governing combat: the victor determines what is considered permissible.

It might seem to you, therefore, that to engage within battle against terrorists represents some form of blood ritual – and you are most emphatically correct in this belief. It *is* a blood ritual with catastrophic implications. Fighting terrorism represents, always remember, basic human *survival* at its most subconscious level. Even the horribly brutal battles of the 'World Wars' of the past century followed mathematical theory with astonishing accuracy.[7] Terrorism and guerrilla

---

[7] Martin Braun, *Differential Equations and Their Applications* (New York: Springer-Verlag, 1993), 405.

warfare, by their nature, are less formularized though I, for one, could easily adapt the 1920s Italian study of predator-prey models worked out to understand the rise in Mediterranean sharks during World War One to today's terrorist groups.[8]They being the sharks and innocent civilians representing the prey. However, let us leave differential equations to the academics and syndicated television heroes.

Armies may be somewhat predictable, but humans are not nearly so and with the onslaught unleashed upon al-Qaeda since the September 11, 2001 attacks in New York City and Washington, jihadist groups have "franchised" into ever smaller, decentralized, and unpredictable units. What this means for you, is that you will more than likely be encountering *individuals* – people who will think, function, and respond in a manner not fully isolated from your own. Or, according to accepted Darwinian Law: "The more similar two species are, the fiercer is the struggle for existence between them."[9] Do not worry, however. You will have your own razor sharp dividing line to keep your own brutality one toe into reality.

Regardless of personal inhibitions, there *is* historical precedence for your emulating the terrorists in intensity , if not in tactics or beliefs. The United States won the Plains Indian Wars of 1865 to 1879 by going head-to-head with the American Indians instead of cozying up to them diplomatically. As General Nelson A. Miles said: "They have been petted and, if that policy is continued, they will furnish

---

[8] Ibid., 443-451.
[9] Ibid., *bc*.

warriors for the next twenty years."[10] General Miles knew of what he spoke and his words resonate today as many politicians and leading civilians attempt to accord *our* Constitutional rights to foreign enemies captured and tried on foreign soil. Miles's thoughts of the situation then – of treating hostiles "more as conquerors than prisoners"[11] – resonates today in court actions over Guantanamo Bay detainees such as 9/11 mastermind, Khalid Sheik Muhammad.

Understand, I am *not* denying the role of hate here in order to make it more palatable to vanquish our enemies.[12] Nor am I denying my own role in *dehumanizing* these thugs for the same result.[13] I merely offer that hate is simply another side of the coin on which love rests and I love America so much that I absolutely *hate anyone* messing with her or targeting her citizens. *Period.* End of discussion. Therefore, I hold no qualms, say, of taking out terrorists before they have a chance to plot, plan, or prepare for our extinction. As the *Catechism of the Catholic Church* so eloquently states:

> **"Nor is it necessary for salvation that a man omit the act of moderate self-defense to avoid killing the other man, since one is bound to take more care of one's own life than of another's.**"[14]

---

[10] Robert L. Utley, "Crook and Miles: Fighting and Feuding on the Indian Frontier," *MHQ: The Quarterly Journal of Military History* (Autumn 1989): 89.

[11] Ibid.

[12] Dave Grossman, *On Killing: The Psychological Cost of Learning to Kill in War and Society* (New York: Back Bay Books, 2009), 80-81.

[13] Ibid., 161.

[14] United States Catholic Conference, Inc. *Catechism of the Catholic Church* (New York: Doubleday, 1994), Paragraph #2264.

"Moderate self-defense" to me represents a double-tap to the Jihadist's head and I, personally, see little problem in facing my Maker on the subject. My argument would be, "If he had not lifted a finger to harm me, then he would still be alive today." I will gladly face the fires of hell for something that *I did* but I will be damned if I am going to fry for what others forced me to do.

Listen, people, our lives are not ours, our nation is not ours, and our freedoms certainly are not ours if we allow someone to take them away from us unopposed. Everything within our society – from our tornado sirens to our police and fire departments and on through the Department of Homeland Security – is based upon the concept of reaction. We need to plan for *action*. If we allow our lives to be governed according to outside influence, whether waiting for the sirens to tell us to seek cover from an approaching twister or having the federal government instruct us on which nations are safe to visit, then we must accept that at *some point*, that influence will become inadequate for *our particular situation*.

I would propose that a fundamental reason that you are reading this book is one of curiosity. That is good, for curiosity helps keep you alive. Just remember that curiosity eventually killed the cat in the fable. What you need to be is *prepared* and so, if you find yourself reading these words, let it become a way of life for you, this obsession with survival. Do not let a day go by without first and foremost thinking of how you can come back home safely at the end of the day. Chance are, for the most part, that you have become accustomed to relying solely upon, well, *chance*. Not anymore, friend.

I want you to be reading this book because you

understand the primal nature of the threat; that we cannot always rely upon our brave men and women in the military or federal government to protect us *one hundred percent* of the time. And your friends and neighbors, if not most of your family, will be hopelessly inadequate to come to your aid during any form of crisis situation.

Before we proceed, I want you to make a promise to *yourself* – not to me, your wife, or Auntie Busty. I want you to promise yourself that you will begin every day of every week of every year reminding yourself of the following words:

> **"The ruling to kill the Americans and their allies – civilian and military – is an individual duty for every Muslim who can do it in any country in which it is possible to do it.."** Sheikh Usamah Bin-Muhammed Bin-Laden and Ayman al-Zawahiri, February 23, 1998.

Bin Laden may be dead – thank God – but Zawahiri and hundreds of thousands of supporters are not, and nearly every one of them have read this *published* decree. Print these words, as well as the following released by Bin Laden's official spokesman nine months after the 9/11/2001 attacks, upon a series of Post-It Notes® and place them where you will be able to read them:

> **"We have the right to kill 4 million Americans – 2 million of them children – and to exile twice as many and wound and cripple hundreds of thousands."** Suleiman

Abu Gheith.[15]

Bin Laden may indeed be dead, but the threat from al-Qaeda has only begun. What confronts us today represents a kaleidoscope of lone wolves and covert cells resembling the Fort Hood massacre suspect, the ill-fated Christmas Day bomber, and the vile murderers of our ambassador in Benghazi during September 11, 2012. Do *not* believe our politicians when they say that the threat has either been diminished because of Bin Laden's death (the Pakistanis have been making noise saying that he was ill and out of the picture anyway and Bin Laden certainly watched enough pornography at his Abbottobad home to suggest this as true), or that al-Qaeda is on the run.

The Islamic Jihadists bear a weapon far more powerful than anything that the United States government has and rears against them and we will discuss this horrendous "technology" within the next chapter. For now, simply understand that *you* too possess this all-encompassing and all-powerful tool. Use it *wisely*.

---

[15] Graham Allison, *Nuclear Terrorism: The Ultimate Preventable Catastrophe* (New York: Times Books, 2004), 12.

3 THE ROLE OF RELIGION IN SURVIVAL.

For most Christian Americans, prayer represents a deeply private affair, even amongst your more vocal fundamentalists who seek to better the world largely through the context of the secular state.[16] For Islamists, however, spiritual life and daily, public life remain inseparable.[17] We, in the West, appear to have outgrown our reliance upon all things "religious" for our daily needs. We have lost this intimate companionship with the divine that existed for nearly 1,300 years until we began to fabricate other "faiths" to fill the void.[18] This de-Christianization of our culture, perhaps more prominent in Great Britain and Europe, has set us up for savage attacks by those who have chosen to more widely embrace their own religious militancy.[19]

Listen to what real, *documented* faith can lead one to do, in this case involving mystic St. Simeon Stylites (390? – 459

---

[16] Fawaz A. Gerges, *Journey of the Jihadist: Inside Muslim Militancy* (Orlando: Harcourt, 2006), 35.

[17] Ibid.

[18] Peter Kreeft, *Everything that you ever wanted to know about Heaven...but never dreamed of asking* (San Francisco: Ignatius Press, 1990), 193.

[19] Ibid.

A.D.) of Syria:

> **"Simeon built himself a column six feet high and lived on it. Ashamed of his moderation, he built and lived on ever taller columns, until he made his permanent abode on a pillar sixty feet high. Its circumference at the top was little more than three feet; a railing kept the saint from falling to the ground in his sleep. On this perch Simeon lived uninterruptedly for thirty years, exposed to rain and sun and cold. A ladder enabled disciples to take him food and remove his waste. He bound himself to the pillar by a rope; the rope became embedded in his flesh, which putrefied around it, stank, and teemed with worms; Simeon picked up the worms that fell from his sores, and replaced them there, saying to them, 'Eat what God has given you.'"[20]**

Imagine hoisting your office chair upon a sixty foot high flagpole and then residing there "uninterruptedly" for *thirty years*.

Since few records ever remain unbroken, Simeon's followers – and there were many, known simply as the Stylites – matched his feat for periods up to *sixty* years in duration. And you cannot sit through your boss's Monday morning lecture without thinking about the coffee pot. Is it any wonder, then, how badly we have lost touch with our

---

[20] Will Durant, *The Age of Faith* (New York: Simon and Schuster, 1950), 60.

own cultural heritage? Could any of the great cathedrals in Europe, many constructed over the course of *centuries*, ever be built within technologically-advanced but hopelessly secularized today? Any community that places even a plaque of the Ten Commandments anywhere in public is immediately slapped with a lawsuit by so-called "Separation of Church and State" individuals who, more often than not, make up a decided minority of the population. What would the ACLU do with a *four-hundred year* public works project to build a single church?

What we are faced with, in our battle against modern Islamic extremists (and quite possibly a significant portion of the overall Muslim population[21]), remains a foe that possesses the gut determination and patience of a Saint Simeon Stylites with the diabolical hatred of an Usama Bin Laden or an Ayman al-Zawahiri. In other words, people who can remain isolated for thirty years and still shout out to the world "Kill Americans! Military *and* civilians! Kill *two million American children!*"

How does the West respond? We blame subsequent attacks, such as that that killed American Ambassador to Libya Chris Stevens and three others in Benghazi on September 11, 2012 as spontaneous demonstrations protesting some obscure YouTube video clip that no one heretofore realized existed. My 85-year-old mother understood that the attack upon our consulate as well as the attack against our Embassy in Cairo represented a terrorist attack. Apparently, our government did not.

---

[21] Many experts believe that radicalized Muslims account for "only" 10-20% of the global Muslim population. Taken at 15%, the figure exceeds the estimates of the total number of combatants during 1939-1945 of ~105,542,100 individuals. Source: John Ellis, *World War II: The Encyclopedia of Facts and Figures* (Military Book Club, 1993), 253-254.

When waging psychological warfare against our opponents – a fundamental element of the war against terrorism – we need to spread *our* message passionately, indulging within color, symbolism, folklore, and the pure emotion of the religiously-tuned human spirit.[22]Historically, the individuals of the world have been challenged by conflicting arguments of *"'It's a horrible idea for you to change your ways...'* and *'Brother, have I got something great in store for you!'"*[23]In this context, it serves no one to try to win 'hearts and minds' without the stomach to back one's pledges up with.

Nevertheless, we tread upon a very slippery slope whenever we rely solely upon religious faith to guide us through the chaotic events upon the battlefield.[24] Many a 16th century individual believed that God would deflect cannonballs and had to turn and flee in horror when projectile physics overpowered prayer on the fields of North-Central Europe.[25] If only we could be as sterilizing in our routing out of ideological fanatics today.

The only role that religious faith should – and *needs* to – serve today remains strictly within the motivational sector. We *need* to be motivated, primarily we citizens, or else our more 'inspired' enemies will gladly blow themselves apart in our midst while our minds are concentrated on sports,

---

[22] Balor, *Mercenary Soldier*, 217.

[23] R.J. Godlewski, "Latte Intelligence: The Divorce of Shock Creativity and Special Information Operations" *American Intelligence Journal* 29 no. 1 (2011): 72.

[24] Billy Waugh and Tim Keown, *Hunting the Jackal: A Special Forces and CIA Soldier's Fifty Years on the Frontlines of the War Against Terrorism* (New York: Avon Books, 2004), 145.

[25] Ralph Peters, "Rebels and Religion: How Fighters become Fanatics," *Armed Forces Journal* (January 2007): 31.

Hollywood, food, and a myriad of other distractions. There is, after all, nothing inherently wrong with shouting, "Hot damn! Praise the Lord! Did you see the tight grouping that I placed between the bastard's eyes?" whenever we are calming down from an attack by a dozen armed assailants. It is when we resort to "Please, dear Lord. Kindly deflect those Katyusha rockets away from me" while we are standing out in the open that things get to be a little dicey.

God does not play favorites with free will. He might tweak the human psyche every now and then or disrupt the natural world, but He does not manhandle the situation. Even Christ acknowledged that people *could* do harm to Him if God the Father permitted it to happen.[26] He knew that when crisis and aggravation bore their ugly heads, there would not be another living soul around prepared to die to save an innocent life. Times have *not* changed any today.

Enemies, you understand, make for strange bedfellows. Common foes unite common enemies. Shia and Sunni Muslims band together to wage war against the West. Sailors and Marines become good friends during the Army-Navy game. Communist China and Islamic jihadists emerge as kindred spirits in the pursuit of opportunity.[27] And progressive liberals join with the Islamists to spoil Christianity around the planet. God, for His divine role, resembles a hovering classroom instructor. He would *like* to nudge us into the correct direction, or perhaps even "sneeze" out the answer, but God knows that the *only* way that we will learn is by solving the problem *ourselves*.

---

[26] John 19:11, *NAB*.

[27] H. John Poole, *Dragon Days: Time for "Unconventional" Tactics* (Emerald Isle, NC: Posterity Press, 2007), 3-23.

Thus for every evil person on the planet that does something terribly wrong, God provides us with thousands upon thousands of individuals that should, conceivably, fill the "Good Samaritan" role. It remains for us to find a way to use those talents, interests, and gifts that He has bestowed upon us to survive within this maddening world of ours. That, friend, is where *you* come into the picture.

You understand that Islamic jihadists want to destroy as many of us as they can. You know that they want to expand a universal caliphate that extends beyond the boundaries that existed in 750 A.D. You see it within their actions – and within their intent – everyday on the television news and Internet. Their actions speak louder than words, even louder than the homicide bombings that destroy weddings, crowded shopping malls, and the gunfire that rips through military command centers and recruiting posts. You realize that from *your perspective*, the only good terrorist is a dead one.

What you might not understand, however, is that if *you* – the concerned citizen with the seven children throwing food at one another during the evening meal – do not do *something* to stem the tide, then nobody else may. There remains a reason, friend, that you are lucky enough to have that nice comfortable home with the seven brats driving your wife insane. For, perhaps, the whole of your life you have been accustomed to placing complete faith in your military, your federal agencies, and your local police departments to protect your ass should the need arise.

Guess what? Economic evolution dictates that as the world grows more populous and competitive, those forces provided by taxpayers will diminish in both size and effectiveness. As terrorists, drug traffickers, and other transnational criminal elements inch ever closer to possessing "death rays" and other weapons of mass destruction, our local and national politicians will continue to dawdle over, say, passing laws acknowledging our natural right to own and bear firearms.

Politicians, simply by virtue of their trade, represent cowards. It remains the truth. They will bend over backwards to accommodate those they fear but will sacrifice those they represent. If you cannot trust that another individual would come to your aid when the need arises, then you certainly *cannot* trust that a politician will see to *your* needs beforehand. This, friend, is where being "religious" definitely comes in handy.

To engage personal survival alone and, frankly, at great odds requires one to be highly motivated and possess a self-confidence that is to be considered rather remarkable within today's day and age. You must not only *anticipate* survival within a wide variety of situations, you must actually *believe* it. This is not very easy, especially when surviving within today's environment requires you to be on your toes one hundred percent of the time. For instance, I preach being engulfed within your 360° sphere of personal awareness as imperative. That said, I understand that after, say, walking eight to ten miles in the sun or other adverse conditions, a person's senses dull. It is just natural.

Therefore, if you cannot present "superhuman capabilities", it helps to be able to call upon superhuman *beliefs*. In other words, religious beliefs *can* provide you with that added spunk or incentive that you need to remain alert when you are getting tired from twenty-mile marches or being shot at. Past martyrs and saints came from little different backgrounds than you probably do, but what made them *special* was how they used their individual faith to bear them through extraordinarily horrendous events. St. Sebastian was pierced repeatedly by arrows unleashed from Mauritanian archers, briefly healed, and had to be eventually clubbed to death. In 17th century Japan, British Captain Richard Cocks saw Christian children as young as five and six years old being burned alive within their mother's arms. Later, in about 1650 A.D., the total number of Christians killed in Japan approximated 200,000 to 300,000 individuals. During the Second World War, Saint Maxmillian Kolbe offered his own life in exchange for a married man with children who was about to be executed within a Nazi concentration camp.

Each one of us believes in *something* greater than him or herself. It might be God, the United States Constitution, or simply "Life, liberty, and the pursuit of happiness." Regardless, it defines what makes us work hard, protect our families, and keep physically and mentally fit. People with a sound purpose rarely represent pathetic souls. Normally. If you consciously choose to go to war against terrorists – an assumption made by your reading these words – then you *must devote your entire life to the endeavor.* Slack for a moment, and the Beast will devour you. Say what you want, but *religious faith* provides you with an added edge; the personal power and integrity that will keep you motivated to "crush, kill, destroy" along with the sanctity to do so only to protect innocent human lives.

There remains a model of human behavior that equates our species with that of canines. In this manner, there exists wolves (sociopaths), packs of wild dogs (gangs and aggressive armies), sheep dogs (soldiers, police officers, and active citizens), and, of course, sheep (everyone else).[28] You have to make a personal and lasting decision of which group that you wish to run with; which "animal" best identifies your truest intent. As for myself, I am proud to aspire with the sheepdogs – I remain friendly, lovable, and loyal, but when aroused I can sink my fangs into even the most vicious wolf in order to protect my clan. My religious faith provides me with this sense of immortal duty.

Sadly, not everyone inhabiting our planet shares this belief. At best, they feel that religion represents an enemy, not a tool to empower the human spirit. At worst, they use *their* religious beliefs to segregate individuals and destroy "infidel" nations. God, for the former group, represents an affront to the human intellect. For the latter, He represents a military commander guiding the righteous towards global domination. Both parties are inherently wrong. God exists for *all* human individuals, even those who consciously choose to deny, ignore or hide from Him.

Both groups, unfortunately, feel that *Christianity* remains the only religious faith unacceptable to the human population. Radicalized Islam appears tolerated by secularists. Remember, however, this remains because secularists often ally themselves with the Islamists and arm your own intentions accordingly. From this point forward, you are either going to be associated with them or you are going to establish yourself as a threat to their agenda. Are you *ready*? Good.

---

[28] David A. Grossman, "Defeating the Enemy's Will: The Psychological Foundations of Maneuver Warfare" in *Maneuver Warfare: An Anthology*, ed. Richard D. Hooker, Jr. (Novato, CA: Presidio Press, 1993), 175.

4 CONDITIONING YOURSELF FOR THE FIGHT OF YOUR LIFE.

N ow that you have decided to take a stand against the terrorists hell-bent on your personal destruction, perhaps it behooves you to take stock of your physical and mental condition. Chances are, you are in far worse shape than you care to admit. All is not lost, however, for the tools that you need to recover the fitness of your youth remain all around you. First, however, we need to work on your mental attitude.

A Warrior's Mind

When confronted with danger, a person has but four distinct options available.[29]

- **Fight**. A person can stand his or her ground and fight the crisis at hand;
- **Posture.** A person can stand his or her ground, but instead of fighting will 'flair up' and present a more

---

[29] Grossman, *On Killing*, 7.

threatening image in the hope that their adversary will capitulate or flee;

- **Flight.** An individual can give ground and make a hasty retreat back towards safety;
- **Submit.** An individual can simply give up and surrender, accepting whatever conditions that the victor may place upon them.

To surrender or run takes little initiative and therefore I will not discuss these two options. The other two − and quite probably combinations of them − represent what needs to be discussed when dealing with terrorists and other criminal elements. Posturing represents, perhaps, the more natural of the two and therefore we shall begin our discussion with it.

Posturing is, quite simply, inflating one's image to compensate for or hide one's physical inabilities. This is what happens when your neighbor's pet Chihuahua begins barking like a Rottweiler whenever you approach their "territory" too closely. You realize that you can stomp the little bugger into the ground without effort, but the dog believes that maybe, just *maybe*, if they act mean and vicious enough, you just might go off into another direction. Humans are not generally so accommodating, so we have to fabricate artificial methods of making ourselves look scary when confronted by our own kind.

Whether the battle cry of a Greek phalanx, the ridiculously inappropriate hats of the Napoleonic era, or the terrifying 'rebel yell' of the Southern Confederacy, people try their best to make themselves appear threatening to their enemies in the hope that *they* will either flee or capitulate.[30] During the Second World War, Germans placed sirens on their Stuka dive bombers to terrify targeted populations, a tactic recorded for posterity within various newsreels from the conflict.

More recent examples of posturing flow from your favorite sports team. Whether from their sideline antics or insistence upon slapping gruesome graffiti all over their arms in the form of tattoos, they try to get the entire planet to know that they remain big, bad-assed athletes who intend to win. Generally, however, they do not. Those that eventually win represent the non-descript players who have actually prepared for the challenge.

Posturing may work for you but I recommend against it unless it is needed, for instance, to cover an escape and evasion effort should you ever find yourself deep behind "enemy lines" even if that merely represents the inner cities of Detroit, New York, Los Angeles, etc. In our case, as an independent counterterrorist operative, posturing may call unwanted attention to your efforts and, without proper backup, you will unnecessarily place yourself and your loved ones in jeopardy. More important for you, obviously, remains the motivation to fight and survive.

Like-species rarely ever turn upon one another for the kill, acquiescing to the primal law designed to prevent extinction. Elk will lock horns and battle one another for hours until one side capitulates, but these same elk will use their racks to devastating effect upon a wolf or a coyote. Humans, on the other hand, have to devise unnatural methods in which to kill one another. We possess our mathematical formulae and

---

[30] Grossman, "Defeating the Enemy's Will," 155.

our scientific equations.[31]However, it has been admirably stated that scientific study of men in combat is like "a world of virgins studying sex, with nothing to go on but porno films."[32]For our purposes, we shall only discuss one particular scientific study that relates to our personal conditioning.

During the 1960s, Dr. Stanley Milgram of Yale University conducted a study involving human obedience and aggressive behavior and discovered that over sixty-five percent (65%) of the human population could be readily manipulated into delivering a "lethal" charge of electricity upon a total stranger.[33] Moreover, these test subjects continued to inflict this torture – even increasing the voltage – until long after the victims would have really been dead.[34] This research has since been validated by subsequent studies within dozens of countries.[35]

What allows people to commit such acts? How can normal, everyday subjects be induced into inflicting such pain upon the innocent? There exist several methods:[36]

- If the person is within proximity to an authority figure, they may be inclined to obey for fear of ridicule or punishment. Conversely, they may be inclined to perform as expected out of fear that should they fail, their leader may be replaced with someone far worse;

---

[31] Braun, *Differential Equations*, 398-414.
[32] Grossman, "Defeating the Enemy's Will," 144.
[33] Ibid.
[34] Ibid.
[35] Ibid.
[36] Grossman, *On Killing*, 187-194.

- If the person is a member of a group, they will perform more effectively for fear of being labeled as the "weakest link". Being within any group also provides the individual with a sense of conformity and accountability;

- Through modern technology, individuals can establish a *physical distance* between themselves and the victims. Nobody thinks twice about seeing images of a B-52 dropping its load over a mountain target, for example, but when that same individual sees images of brutal, hand-to-hand fighting within a major city, they more fully understand the devastation of war. The further they remain from their target – through the use of hand grenades to rifles on through artillery and long-range aircraft – their resistance towards killing dissolves proportionately;

- Individuals can also increase the *emotional distance* between them and their victim, employing hate (such as that towards ethnic, religious, or racial differences, etc.) to *dehumanize* victims, thus making it far easier to kill. This is the technique employed to get gullible young Muslims to murder "infidels" en masse; the combination of Westerners representing non-Muslim individuals and the tempting reward of paradise persuades them to commit the unthinkable. Individuals can also increase the emotional separation from victims by shielding their faces or shooting them in the back of the head where the victim's eyes do not suggest humanity and concern.

You, in your independent efforts to combat terrorism, will be lacking in proximity to any authoritative figure as well as the benefits of group camaraderie. This is one reason why we discussed religion previously; a religious element within your life can – and should – provide you with a sense of both. Religion – of whatever personal choice – can provide you with an authority figure to follow, and be afraid of angering. It can also provide you with an established doctrine followed by millions of believers around the world. In decidedly Christian America, this choice of adherence is easy.[37]

Christianity remains part of our American heritage, our communities, and undoubtedly part of our families. Our founding fathers not only invoked God in nearly every document they produced, they used Christian doctrine in formulating our path towards independence. We may not wish to reflect upon this and God knows that in our ultra-politically correct world, religion remains very much taboo – specifically Christianity – but facts remain facts. George Washington, our very first president, declared it to be quite "impossible to rightly govern a nation without God and the Bible". If only Washington the city were as devoted as Washington the man.

I suspect, however, that you are reading these words because you do not care very much about what others may think. You understand that Islamic jihadists have targeted

---

[37] The U.S. Central Intelligence Agency (CIA) places the Christian population at ~ 76.8%. See https://www.cia.gov/library/publications/the-world-factbook/geos/us.html. Accessed October, 2012. Adherents.com places this figure at ~ 82%. See http://www.adherents.com/rel_USA.html. Accessed October, 2012.

Americans and other Westerners for death. You know that the narco cartels remain on the verge of destroying Mexico and, perhaps, sending millions of "narco-refugees" fleeing north for the semblance of security within the United States.[38]You understand that these various groups will not stop until they *are* stopped and that you realize that military and federal resources remain finite in scope. Thus, you have decided that *you* must become a solution to the problem and want to do something to protect yourself and your loved ones from these vile thugs masquerading as legitimate human beings. Well, compadre, chances are that you are doing so from a religious perspective.

If you desire to make a stand against both Islamic, narco, and political terrorism, I am willing to bet that you are doing so because of one or more of the following reasons:

- You do not want anyone enforcing their beliefs upon you;

- You do not subscribe to the beliefs that others are trying to force upon you;

- You believe that all people were *created* equal and are possessing of certain inalienable rights;

- You detest the use of indiscriminate violence against innocents as a means of affecting political change;

- You believe within established law and order as determined by duly elected and/or appointed officials determined by the citizenry;

---

[38] Paul Rexton Kan, *Mexico's "Narco-Refugees": The Looming Challenge for U.S. National Security* (Carlisle, PA: Strategic Studies Institute, October 2011), 25-29.

- You value your life above all others, with the possible exception of your spouse and family;

- You believe that it remains individuals and families, not governments or political leaders, which form the foundation of society.

Whether you care to admit it or not, *all* of these came to be as the result of religious beliefs – specifically Western Judeo-Christian beliefs. Furthermore, religion can provide the independent a sense of companionship to fall back upon during trying times. Again, knowing that millions of Christian martyrs had suffered through often worse things before may aid you in understanding the inherent power within your own faith while you are being targeted by, say, fanatical Islamists. Also, remaining in communion with an established set of beliefs – for example, the 2,000 year tradition of the Roman Catholic Mass has remained virtually unaltered since before Saint Justin explained the proceedings to pagan emperor Antoninus Pius around the year 155 A.D. – provides you with an infinitely larger group of people who may support your efforts.

Knowing that you represent, in the case of Christianity, only one of over a billion and a half "non-Islamists", will help you corral the most powerful tool ever invented for waging war – raw hatred. Ironically, this represents our downfall in Western, Christian culture – we allow ourselves to be repeatedly attacked because we just cannot understand how "some" people can actually hate one another to do the sort of things that terrorists and other criminals do. Let us leave that to psychologists and sociologists to debate. For you, however, just be thankful that humans *can* hate.

I consider myself to be just as loving and as compassionate as the next person. I want to defeat cancer, build schools in Asia, provide healthcare to Africa, and spread economic development in Eastern Europe. Still, like the loyal and devoted sheepdog, I can become extremely vicious when my "flock" is threatened. That is, I absolutely *hate* tyrants, terrorists, and transnational criminals. I do not particularly care what religion they practice, what system of beliefs they endorse, or even what nationality or ethnic group they come from.

If you threaten me or mine, I will hurt you *severely* or die in the process of trying. I will use a combat knife to rip your throat out, an elephant gun to tear your head off, or a "death ray" to send your clan back into the stone age never to be found by any future anthropologist. How can I make such claims? Because I absolutely, positively *hate* people who prey upon unsuspecting innocents. Yes, we all remain a little devious or perhaps disingenuous, but I am not talking about the neighbor who forgets to return your garden shears or the kid that breaks into the house across the street to steal Playboy® magazines for his older brother (guilty as charged, I might add).

When it comes to terrorists, I , for one, do not classify them as *human* and I am not afraid to admit as much. What kind of father plans his death in a homicide bombing to kill non-aggressive soldiers and what kind of mother permits their four-year-old son to continuously watch the videotape of the child's father killing himself?[39] That child is unlikely to grow up to become anything but another homicide bomber with a complete disregard for innocent human life. It is

---

[39] Hala Jaber, *Hezbollah: Born With a Vengeance* (New York: Colombia University Press, 1997), 1.

because I consider "human" to be a form of office that I can make such distinctions. For instance, a spirit may either be an angel or a demon depending upon their specific nature and the office they may or may not hold. In this regard, not all *Homo sapiens* should be considered as *human*. Religious beliefs aside, I do not waste time equating an Usama Bin Laden or an Ayman al-Zawahiri with either Mother Theresa or the Dalai Lama. Yes, each professed a certain religious belief and, yes, each represented a member of the *H. sapiens* species. The difference remains that I would gladly donate to Mother Theresa's surviving organization or tip my hat to the Dalai Lama and his followers, but would just *love* to see al-Qaeda and related Islamist groups nuked into non-existence.

What you, the budding independent counterterrorist, must *not* do, however, is become all-consumed by hate alone. You must ensure that the flipside of the emotion – love – remains fully extended to your fellow man. Do not profess killing terrorists for the sake of killing fellow people. Strive to protect the *innocent* instead. The terrorists *are* consumed by hatred. They *do* want to kill for the sake of killing. You are much better than that.

You desire to serve life, even if just your own. They want life to serve them, and there is a distinction just as there is a distinction between your viciousness and theirs. Remember, we are talking about sheepdogs and wolves here. One attacks unprovoked; the other merely defends. When left alone, there remains little to differentiate the sheepdog from their attendant flock.

You may also note that there is usually a single sheepdog attending that flock, not an "army" of dogs or battalions. Just one. It may even surprise you that, historically, it has been private enterprise that first offered protection against the terrorists and that taxpayer-funded "official" forces developed from them.[40]Regardless, individuals "have a perfect right to protect themselves, or to hire people to protect them and their property."[41]It has always been that way in our country, so you are not doing anything particularly new here.

What makes you a breath of fresh air is that the vast majority of your neighbors have opted out for remaining sheep. We – you and I and our compatriots – are tired of having wool pulled over our eyes. We see the Islamists targeting America. We see the Muslim *ummah* shamefully silent on the issue. We see the narcotics cartels continually disregarding our borders and our sovereignty. We see the political leadership in Washington, too, shamefully silent on the issue. We understand that *something* must be done to protect our lives even if it means actually going to war against the terrorists ourselves.

A Warrior's Body

Now that your mind is beginning to see through the clutter of inept political bodies and apathetic communities, it is time to get your body up to snuff. No need to fear, even nice middle-class kids emerge from self-imposed training regimens with the capacity to slit throats with great ease.[42]Of course, *that* might be just a wee bit too drastic for you – until someone tries to murder your son or rape your teenage daughter. Then, by all means, rip their innards to shreds.

---

[40] Christopher Dobson and Ronald Payne, *Counterattack: The West's Battle Against the Terrorists* (New York: Facts on File, 1982), 163.
[41] Ibid., 164.
[42] Balor, *Mercenary Soldier*, 84.

It is *not* my intention within this book to teach you to kill – or even *tell* you to kill. That is not what I am all about. Only *you* can decide what needs to be done during any particular moment or crisis. Already, far too many people are out there providing you with conflicting suggestions and recommendations beyond what needs to be discussed. First of all, however, you will probably have your hands full simply whipping your body back into shape.

There is only *one* thing that is keeping you from having a body in good shape: excuses. Similarly, there is only one thing that is keeping you from possessing a body in *great* shape: lack of effort. For starters, let us work towards the first step in getting you on your way to leading commando operations against hardened terrorists – getting you off of your sofa and away from the television. Inactivity can add *twenty* pounds to even the most conscientious individual. I know, because this represents the exact amount that I gained when I ceased walking four miles each way to town (when on Sundays, in a suit and tie with dress boots no less) and returned to full-time university studies.

You can still partake of cheeseburgers, pizza, brownies, cheesecake, etc. and just about anything else that you wish to devour. The point is, however, to take things in moderation. No need to "Super Size" everything. I, for instance, may eat two cheeseburgers for evening meal, but might skip lunch or eat something simple such as a banana. Chicken stir-fries are good, especially since you can load the meal with peppers and other ingredients (I add sautéed mushrooms and avocado to the mix). My favorite dish is a layered creation where I mix ground chicken or turkey with white rice that I have made using the juice from black olives instead of water and diced black olives. Spread out onto a baking pan, I layer sliced bell peppers, Poblano peppers, sliced bananas, avocado chunks, and altering layers of pepper jack and cheddar cheese. The meat is marinated in Bourbon peppercorn sauce and tequila lime sauce is poured over the entire dish before placing into the oven for about an hour. Served hot with a dousing of tarragon vinegar, the meal is delicious, filling, and surprisingly not fattening, but I digress...

Eating healthy is only part of the equation; you must burn off the excess fat and calories and that involves physical exercise. You will be going up against people who in turn are able to stand up against fatigue, hunger, and thirst; know how to hide and be vigilant; have mastered the art of dissembling; have learned to never fear danger; and have learned to function the same whether in day or night, mountains or desert, woodlands or jungle.[43] For now, your greatest fear is going through the day with less food.

Relax, you are a long way from grabbing your AR-type rifle with the fourth-generation night vision scope and heading off to the southern border of the United States to stalk illegal aliens. That *might* come later. Presently, you need to shed some weight and beef some muscles. At least exercise will not set you back $10,000 for tactical equipment. In fact, the whole premise of this book is to get you to do extraordinary things with what is already available to you.

For starters, stop drinking fattening things such as regular sodas. I lost several pounds by shifting to Coke Zero®, which, I am astonished to say, now tastes better than regular Coke®. The only difference being a decided lack of a vanilla flavor, but I have learned to live with that; I detest anything

---

[43] Ibid., 80.

that leaves an aftertaste. More weight can be discharged from your bulk simply through walking. Use the stairs at work, park a bit further from the door at the store, go shopping on foot if you reside only a mile or two from the store. However you choose to do it, keep your feet *moving* through the day and the pounds will come off.

Of course, before you begin *any* strenuous regimen – and, eventually, you will be pumping iron, running lengthy distances, and otherwise conditioning yourself to break bones with little effort -- you need to consult a physician to figure out what your particular limitations are.[44] Until you move into more aggressive training, simply use what Mother Nature has provided you with. Learn to use your *natural environment* to condition your muscles and reflexes.

Treadmills, stair climbers, etc. not only prevent you from conditioning your balance, they also prevent you from conditioning your tactical mind to your environment. When you walk and run, you should be *listening* to the sounds of both your body and your location so that you can learn to dismiss the former and extract threats from the latter. This means, people, do *not* listen to your favorite tunes on your iPod® while exercising. Why would *anyone* in his or her right mind intentionally flood their ears with noise while they are jogging alongside the road?

If you want to survive within this world of ours, you must *always* pay attention to your 360° sphere of personal awareness. What this means, is that as you drive along State Highway 33 you are constantly aware of what rest not

---

[44] Mark De Lisle, *Special Ops Fitness Training: High-Intensity Workouts of Navy SEALs, Delta Force, Marine Force Recon and Army Rangers* (Berkeley: Ulysses Press, 2008), 18-19.

only in front and behind you, but to the sides as well. That deer should not come within 300 meters of your vehicle before you notice its presence. All of a sudden plowing into a buck at 80 m.p.h. is not going to keep you safe in this world. Now back to exercising...

Your entire body-mind "soul" must work *together* and therefore you cannot segregate physical exercise from work or learning from all activities. At home, when you need to go upstairs, sprint up the steps (being extra cautious if you still have carpet on the steps). A trick that I learned from Sara, rest her soul, was to exercise while doing mediocre chores around the home. Listen, we all have to do boring things around the house every day, such as vacuuming the floor, raking the leaves, doing the dishes, or scrubbing the bathtub. We can build muscles while doing these omnipresent tasks. Practice stretching whenever you rake the leaves or sweep the floor. Do the "wax on, wax off Grasshopper" routine from *The Karate Kid* whenever you scrub the floor or the bottom of your moldy bathtub. Always *plan* physical exercises whenever you have to do routine activities!

The entire principle of cross-training is that all of your muscles are interconnected and, should you have an arm or leg within a cast, the strengthening of your uninjured appendage will benefit the disabled limb. Therefore, whenever you do your walking, take advantage of the asymmetrical environment of hills, curves, bumps, and other obstacles to fortify your sense of balance. When you run, alternate your rhythm by adding short bursts of *speed* in with your jogs. Learn to *sprint* even after you have run for several miles. Try never to permit repetition to become habit unless you are, say, conditioning your quick-draw instinctive shooting.

Improvisational exercises can do wonders as well. While you are awaiting an email or telephone call, use the armrests of your office chair to lift your body upwards several times, building your arm muscles in the process. When near a doorway, use the aperture for isometric exercise. *Any* use of a stationary object to press against utilizes your body weight to great advantage.

The use of small, ten-pound dumbbells will strengthen your arms immeasurably, even if you only do a few reps per day while watching television (*always* the news, or some documentary on war, international affairs, or military tactics!). Hold a weight in each arm as if you were carrying your rifle. This will condition you to actually bear your firearm for extended periods without fatigue.

Swimming remains the *single greatest exercise* of which anyone can partake of. In Hawaii during my more youthful Navy days, I struggled to run a mile per day. After six months of scuba diving, I was able to dash off ten miles per day and sprint the final 300 yards along the peer faster than I had ever been able to run before. If you are fortunate enough to live near the water – a lake, a river, the ocean – *take advantage* of the situation. If you own a pool or even have access to one at a school or fitness club, then *spend more time swimming* than within any other physical activity.

These represent the most *miniscule* of suggestions as this book was never meant to provide an all-inclusive training guide. It remains *your fundamental responsibility* to discover how to turn yourself, not as much into Rambo, but less as Gomer Pyle. The next chapter will require you to be in your best condition – both mentally *and* physically.

5 MARTIAL ARTS TRAINING.

Yours represents a field where people just love to go at each other, one-on-one with their bare hands. Therefore, you will ultimately have to learn to defend yourself with little more than what God has provided you with. Selecting a suitable martial arts training program is a little dicey to say the least. Personally, I have qualms over practicing for something that I would rather dispense with a .45 ACP round. Then there are the many martial arts techniques that bear more resemblance to fencing than actual kill-before-you-are-killed physical combat. You will need to select a program that will stress self-discipline, preparation for physical contact and engagement, speed and coordination of mind and body, and tactics.[45]

What you need to develop is the ability to launch into attack from *any set position* and respond to any threat. You cannot do that if you waste precious moments going into a series of preconfigured stances. You will be dead long before you even think of announcing, "On guard!" Your need

---

[45] Balor, *Mercenary Soldier*, 89-93.

to develop a strong martial arts capability is to kill or subdue an enemy should the need arise, *not* to score points from a judge or audience. Therefore, you need to become fully *digital* in your actions. On, off. Kill and destroy; or pack the kids off to school. *Nothing* in-between. You are either the calm, pleasant family man or you are the most lethal badass on the planet, depending upon what situation that you find yourself within at any given moment in time.

The main thing to remember when choosing a martial arts school or instructor is to stay away from the "sports" programs. I say this because of two fundamental facts: 1. A black belt only guarantees that your pants will not fall down; and 2. I know of instances where female martial arts "experts" were brutally raped and their male counterparts savagely killed by *untrained* losers. You need to develop the most lethal hand-to-hand combat system that you can learn within the shortest time available. Nothing less than the most destructive weapon should ever be contained within your personal arsenal – and that includes knowledge of unarmed combat. Add to this the unnerving thought that if you *wait* until defense is required, your life may have already been effectively extinguished.

Imagine, for a moment, if you were to round a corner within a crowded shopping mall and found yourself confronted with a terrorist about to detonate a bomb. Are you comfortable enough with your chosen discipline to neutralize the bomber before he or she has had time to detonate the explosives? Or would you waste precious seconds going into some pre-packaged motion instilled within your psyche through months, if not years, of hierarchal training? If you cannot take down an assailant, however armed or sized, with one quick strike then your karate preference is a waste.

Period.

Before moving onto the next chapter, I would like to discuss two "programs" worthy of study, both personally and through appropriate, professional training. The first involves Ninjutsu – the ancient art of the Ninja and perhaps the best martial arts system for the warrior operating within the bush.[46]Diverting a bit, perhaps, from the *mechanics* involved in neutralizing an enemy, this system teaches the ability to remain concealed and stealthy in your movements. Who needs rhino-powerful strikes when you can sneak up on your enemy and slit their throat and haul ass away before their heart attempts another beat? Ninja – the ancient trade practiced by those who were boiled alive in hot oil if they were caught, not the modernistic interpretation practiced by trendy Hollywood actors and their aquatic characters – represents more of a way of life than nearly every other martial arts package. You would do well to study its foundations.

The second "program" of note represents the modern emergence of Mixed Martial Arts (MMA) an exploding phenomenon around the planet. Mixed martial arts, perhaps rightfully so, embodies "the most complex form of combat known to man" involving "many disciplines, including boxing, wrestling, muay thai, judo, and Brazilian Jiu Jitsu."[47] MMA is certainly not a style to be discovered through a few weekend lessons or gazing upon a few matches on television, but should be integrated into your lifelong – repeat, *lifelong* – commitment to defeating terrorists.

---

[46] James W. England, *Long-Range Patrol Operations: Reconnaissance, Combat, and Special Operations* (Boulder: Paladin Press, 1987), 255.
[47] Martin Rooney, *Training for Warriors: The Ultimate Mixed Martial Arts Workout* (New York: Collins, 2008), 11.

The ingenuity of the style, however, remains the beauty of employing maneuvers to counter any threat's actions. Anything that evolved from an "original bare-knuckled, no-holds-barred, tournament" cannot be all that bad for the objective counterterrorist.[48] As a warrior, you must employ every technique imaginable to ensure your safety and the demise of your enemy. The old Soviet KGB, for example, held few qualms about producing field manuals for their Alpha teams depicting the brutal killing of American Airborne and Special Forces soldiers.[49]While the United States practiced with paper targets and hay-filled dummies, the Soviets knew precisely who their enemy was. Do not *ever* let civility or, today, political correctness stand in the way of vanquishing your enemies.

If you are going to survive within this rapidly threatening world of ours, especially one where you are going to confront people quite willing to exchange their lives for yours, then you are definitely going to have to develop your psychic sensitivity.[50]You may not be aware of it, but you bear the ability to detect a threat from the mere glance of a person's eyes, gauge an individual's heartbeat through your own hearing, and even decipher a person's health through the color of their skin.[51] Where you may find these capabilities "miraculous" rests because ten thousand years of civilization have distanced our minds from the ravages of the Serengeti. In other words, you would probably forget how to breathe, too, if some machine provided that service to you.

---

[48] Ibid., 5.

[49] Paladin Press, *KGB Alpha Team Training Manual: How the Soviets Trained for Personal Combat, Assassination, and Subversion* trans. Jim Shortt (Boulder: Paladin Press, 1993), 217.

[50] England, *Long-Range Patrol*, 255.

[51] R.J. Godlewski, "Human Intelligence: Perceiving an Enemy's Thoughts," *American Intelligence Journal* 27 no. 1 ((2009): 29-37.

We in the modern world have simply lost our natural ways and you are going to have to find some method of getting them back. Chances are, you are totally lost even within your local environment. You move through a sea of people, vehicles, thoughts, responsibilities, and aspirations and I bet that you cannot separate a single one of them long enough to employ all five of your senses let alone hope to develop a "sixth".

In the bush, not being able to corral your senses is tantamount to a death sentence and death is what this book is all for delaying. At least until you are a ripe old cuss begging for the trumpets of Saint Peter. Away from the trappings of modern conveniences, which are nothing more than distractions, your natural sensors will soon notice things that you never realized that you could detect. You will begin to notice that cigarette smoke can be detected from up to a quarter of a mile away if you are a non-smoker.[52] You will also be able to detect food, cooking fires, even "bathroom" provisions from several hundred meters away.[53] If you do not us toiletries – *why* would you wear cologne or perfume in the bush? – you would be able to detect aftershave, soaps, and over such "luxuries" from considerable distances.[54] Now here rests the real kicker; *you* would not notice these things without having spent a considerable amount of time within, say, the jungle, but someone who had *already* developed these senses can employ them within *your* natural environment.

That is right; you are walking down the street through some Third World cesspool and a potential assailant can

---

[52] England, *Long-Range Patrol*, 255.
[53] Ibid.
[54] Ibid.

smell you, Joe Modern Westerner, coming from a mile away. You do not even have to be in Benghazi to be targeted,[55]half of the people who prey on people in crowded shopping malls stalk their victims employing these same abilities. They gauge you by your own mannerisms, predictabilities, and absentmindedness. My own mother once had her purse lifted from a shopping cart as she was momentarily distracted by a grandchild. What took the thief seconds to achieve, cost my mother three weeks' aggravation in closing credit cards, stopping checks, etc.

You may not ever find the need to take down an armed assailant – I would not rule it out, but the odds may be in your favor – but you can certainly bet that you need to become more concealed within your environment. Therefore, while you are building your macho image through MMA, study the abilities and history of the ancient Ninja groups and apply them to your personal needs.

Learn to employ your hands, not as appendages or even as weapons, but as sensors. Use them to *see* through touch alone. Use your ears to guide you around the commonplace so that you will be able to fall back upon them if your eyes are injured or incapacitated. I was about sixteen the last time that my own eyes were 20/20 unaided, so when I finally realized that my vision was less than perfect – something hard to understand when you have not anything with which to compare your abilities – I waited until I entered the Navy before I received eyeglasses.

The world of difference was so immediately spectacular,

---

[55] In the 2008 version of this book, I used Benghazi as a random location. Last month, on September 11, 2012, our ambassador and three other Americans were killed within that city by organized terrorists. Threats do not change.

that I protected my eyeglasses as if they were the finest china. I simply never wore them while aboard my first ship, preferring to go through eight, ten, even *forty-eight* hour shifts with limited vision rather than risk wrecking my precious eyeglasses for all-important "liberty time". This was not an easy task to accomplish, especially when you had to stand electrical switchboard watches within a 140° F. engine room and pay close attention to hundreds of gauges and dials with the closest being some several feet away.

When my eyes began to go bad, my hearing naturally had to pick up the slack and before long I began to hear the distinct sound made by the whining steam generators. After roaring at several thousand revolutions day in and day out, I could detect even the *slightest* change in speed that announced the pending loss of a generator. The change in pitch was so unmistakable, that I learned to judge my actions more by my ears than the millions of dollars of equipment that the U.S. Navy deemed necessary.

Later, about the time that I had reached my third warship, my insistence upon protecting my precious eyeglasses dissipated with maturity. Sweat could be wiped off, dirt could be scrubbed away, and scratches, well, nobody had yet invented a practical way of keeping scratches off of lenses when working aboard a WWII-surplus vessel. Therefore, I had begun to wear my glasses just like everyone else did. However, my *ears* still remained in perfect – and tuned – working condition.

When we began to lose a generator aboard my new ship, I was able to inform the machinist mates *long* before their own instruments finally informed them of the changes. I heard the generators whine down, the unmistakable change in pitch of a turbine that was slowing. Sure enough, the generator eventually tripped offline and the machinists, who were responsible for the mechanical elements, were sent scurrying to secure them before major damage occurred while a "mere" electrician smiled with that trademark "I *told* you guys so!" smirk of his.

To develop this same trait within yourself, I suggest spending some time going around your home blindfolded. Just sit quietly on the sofa with your eyes closed if you are still not convinced. Before you realize it, your very own ears will begin to detect sounds and noises (there is a difference between the two!) that you never thought possible to hear. *That* capability may save your life someday more than punching through bricks or two-by-sixes.

6 KNOW THY ENEMY.

Before we delve into the sinister world of terrorists and transnational criminals, we need to pause for a moment and reflect upon *who* you are as an individual. Are you reading this book simply because you desire to act macho and fantasize about traveling the world and killing terrorists? Or are you simply preparing yourself for a chance encounter with someone who will ultimately irreparably alter your life forever? If you represent the first motive, then please set this book down and find one more conducive to your barbarism. It has *never* been my intention to teach you to kill or maim. That kind of individual represents precisely *whom* we are trying to defeat. If you are honest with yourself and approach the second motive, then you *still* have to address your fundamental humanity. For this, we need to step back for a moment and see how far each one of us blurs the distinction.

Consider the following scenario very carefully:

Two brutal-looking thugs are in the process of raping your wife or your young, pre-teenage daughter and you have a choice between a cell phone with which to call 911 or a .12 gauge Remington shotgun. Which do you choose? Tough decision, right?

I am willing to bet that the vast majority of you out there – including your more pathetically liberal types – would make straightaway for the shotgun even though more people know how to work the cell phone. This leads directly to another scenario: *what* to do with the gun once it is within your hands? I will hazard a guess and say that roughly 90% of the population will only to threaten to shoot or otherwise command the individuals to cease and desist. The remaining 10% would probably shoot the bastards anywhere from the chest on upwards.

Myself? I would take out their kneecaps. This little gruesome action would serve two distinct functions. First, it would keep them alive just long enough to think. Second, it would give them something to think about. Of course, my brief reflection upon the darker side of human nature was not meant to send the squeamish hauling off to the nearest trash receptacle to vomit. My intent served two purposes. First, it provided you an honest perspective of my natural, gut reaction. This is important; all humans grow aggressive during moments of extreme prejudice, as politicians are wont to say. Secondly, and most importantly, I presented a strong case for educating yourself on *what* to do, *when* to do it, and what to *do it with* for whatever situation you may find yourself confronted with. In other words, *learning* – that despicable word that most of us leave behind in high school or college and university classrooms.

My scenario thus serves another profound purpose; the "choice" inherent within the above presents strictly a *classroom*-type problem. In reality, *no one* should even consider the cell phone for it would do very little to prevent the rape from actually taking place. Your actions must be instantaneous; your thoughts spontaneous. Both the shotgun and the cell phone simply represent *tools*, but only one would work well within that terrible situation.

So where, precisely, would you find the shotgun, you ask? Well, if the studious could imagine the .12 gauge shotgun shrunk down to a .45 caliber pistol and the preparatory would place it within a belt or shoulder holster, then the entire scenario would work out to satisfaction for the consciously trained. This takes foresight, yes, but also requires one to learn. For instance, how did you determine that a .45 round would be more practical than, say, a 9mm? What type of ammunition did you have loaded into your pistol in the first place? How much *practice* and training did you place into using said firearm?

Next, you had to have considered *where* would you have placed your shots to ensure that the rapists were taken down without harming the victim or innocent bystanders. Far more importantly, *what* should you being doing *now* once you saved your wife or daughter (hint: the police are initially going to characterize *you* as the immediate threat)? And you thought that adults had very little to learn about life.

The truth is, sadly, *everything* that you have probably learned since birth ill-prepares you for your new battle against terrorists and hardened criminals. This is not to say that you have wasted your life – indeed, many things that you have already learned or experienced provide you with a distinct advantage over others – just that your mental and emotional disposition have been tainted by Western culture.

I just remains the way that we are – for now.

Our brains have been rewired to accept conditions that remain quite unnatural and detrimental to our survival. Thoughts such as "give your money to the thieves; your life is far more important than mere material possessions" cloud our judgment due to their convincing rationale. Yet, human evolution matured away from the plains of Equatorial Africa where "giving away" things required for survival meant certain extinction. Back then, our ancestors fought back lest they starve and today our subconscious mind struggles to teach us these lessons from, perhaps, millions of years of trial and error.

At their most primal level, threats are perceived to be just that – threats – and we are thus forced with only the four options of which we have already spoken. Those that fight or flee remain around for another day whereas those that submit or stand transfixed in posture mode are readily vanquished by those who bear a definite *need*. Eventually, those that continuously flee come upon a situation where flight is blocked and those that fight may come across a more formidable adversary. It goes without saying, therefore, that the *survivors* of the bunch are those who *continually evolve as fighters*.

Time for your personal rediscovery...

Music, I am told, represents the universal language. Whether this remains true or not, I just know that it still represents many dialects. For example, by temperament, I am a 1960s/1970s rock and roller. There is just *something* about the raw power of the J. Geils Band that propels me to new heights of creativity, for instance. Yet, as I wrote the original version of these words, I was surrounded by the mystical sound of the Benedictine Monks of Santo Domingo De Silos' Gregorian chant. I found their ageless "medieval plainsong" soothing and beneficial in my own art of the written word.

What this says about me, of course, is that I am neither rigid nor fixed within my mannerisms. In other words, I am very much a complicated individual who cannot be defined through stereotypes. I find this to be quite apropos – being a proponent of combating terrorism requires one to be simultaneously compassionate and lethal. The sheepdog that can thump his hind leg against the floor when being scratched behind the ear, but sink its fangs into a much larger foe should the need arise.

You cannot be a simpleton to wage war effectively. Neither can you afford to remain predictable or live according to established patterns. This remains the fundamental reason why classroom leaves much to be desired. I personally know of honors students who fail miserably within the real world environment. Why did they do so well in school and yet collapse miserably outside the classroom? Because their minds were conditioned along the rote-learning methods of academia and therefore their thought processes hardwired to understand the expectations and formulas of classroom predictability.[56] I know of *few* academic institutions that really, *truly* change their methods of instruction from one period to another.

You, on the other hand, cannot take things for granted. September 11th, 2001 happened because we could not imagine airliners flying into crowded office buildings. Yet,

---

[56] Robert D. Steele, *Human Intelligence: All Humans, All Minds, All the Time* (Carlisle, PA: Strategic Studies Institute, 2010), 12.

when a B-25 bomber had inadvertently crashed into the Empire State Building back on July 28th, 1945 more people should have considered 'what if?" Still, we sat and watched dumbfounded when a bunch of young Arab men perpetrated the most heinous crime imaginable. We have not changed much in the interim, believe me.

The difficulties in changing patterns abruptly remains because we notice such changes instantaneously – our subconscious learning process at work. It is the same whenever we move into a new home or perhaps just visit a friend or relative's. Those strange, quirky sounds at night that keep your mind attempting to understand that which is "foreign" to your experiences. Within your own humble abode, you are constantly acknowledging the furnace, the water heater, the wind, settling, or a host of other normal occurrences that experience has long since translated as insignificant. You do not notice these things because they have already been filed away as *unimportant* before your conscious mind even has the time to investigate them.

Much the same rests with your learning processes – you do not learn anything new unless your daily routine is abruptly inconvenienced. That is, you do not learn unless you are forced to discover the "new". Simply sitting around a classroom table playing paper football with your buddy while the professor's back is turned away is not gaining credible knowledge of *anything*. In the *outside* world with the situation involving a corporate environment, you would never really know if your lackadaisical efforts to remain amused were not be recorded by your company's hidden security cameras. Best remain focused from the moment that you first open your eyes in the morning, friend.

Since your primary objective remains to survive an encounter with terrorists – if this is *not* your primary objective, then please go out into the street and wait for the first garbage truck to mow you down; it will accomplish the same result without you having had wasted your time reading this far along – you need to structure your knowledge acquisition within a more profitable manner that forces you to *learn* rather than forever being *educated*.

Let us begin with taking notes – a usual method of recording information whether within a training environment or within the activities of your daily professional life. Chances are that you write down notes in the same manner as you read – here in America, that means writing from left to right and from top on down. Unfortunately, because of the nature of the human mind, you will subconsciously determine quite automatically that the *first* things that your eyes come across represent the most important. Suppose, however, that something noted towards the bottom right of your page contained information that would ultimately save your life?

In order to force your mind to give equal consideration to *all* information regardless of how large your paper is, begin taking notes through inconsistent methods of writing. Write both diagonally and vertically. Use different sizes of script or colors of pens. Forego colloquial English in favor of shorthand scribbling – decipherable symbols that you have invented for just such a purpose. Arrange your notes within a haphazard manner all around the page. What this does, is force your mind to concentrate on *every* note written down as you are required to stop, look, and pay attention to what does not appear "natural" to your lifelong process of reading. You retain the pertinent information because you have not ruled it out as "unimportant" before you actually realize what it really represents.

Now that you have managed to shake yourself free of conventional learning processes – and truly *knowing* thyself – you can now begin applying that ability towards your counterterrorism role. You must begin to *understand* the threat aligned against us and formulate an educational plan that will provide you with an advantage over them.

Your enemies, of course, represent the terrorists, but can you adequately *define* terrorism? Many an academic and political soul have fought over what truly constitutes terrorism and terrorists for years, but for the purposes of this book, we shall employ my own personal definition:

> "I believe that a consensus can be found that would categorize terrorists as private or state-sponsored groups operating largely outside the control of the national military whose fundamental goal is to intimidate people and their governments into recognizing the group's ideologies and/or religious beliefs through the coordinated use of indiscriminate murder, torture, and the destruction of private and public properties, especially that which will achieve a great deal of attention by local and international media organizations. Therefore, this is how I generally define terrorists and anybody who aids them in any manner whatsoever is a terrorist supporter."[57]

We can, quite safely, define our modern terrorist enemies further by revealing them to either be Islamist radicals or narco-terrorists, but we must always be extremely cautious that parties allied with their hatred of us do not buck the

---

[57] R.J. Godlewski, *Integrated Technical Warfare: An Organizational Guide to Creating a Corporate Counterterrorism Force* (Houghton Lake, MI: Road Sailor Books, 2006), 91-92.

trend as it were.[58]We simply do not know from whence a threat to our existence may come and therefore we must always understand that terrorism remains a tool, and *not* specifically a group of individuals. This requires examining the terrorist model from the historical context.

The Socialist/Anarchist Model

For convenience, two similar models have been combined. Their commonality in the form of "anti-democratic" purpose leads to their indistinguishable classification on my part as well as their equally common historical lineage. That is, both socialists and anarchists desire to dismantle the status quo in an effort to change the *existing political system* of their target body. Of the two, only the socialists generally care enough to anticipate an alternative to the current condition of their host nation. Still, they are not beyond using the services of the anarchists to quicken such a change much as Adolf Hitler did during the 1930s. The 21st century version of this could quite possibly represent the various "Occupy" movements that began cluttering Wall Street for perceived economic injustices. *Who* swells within the cloud of popularity may not always represent the cause itself.

Anarchists, for their part, are more liable to orchestrate their trade via "Propaganda by Deed"; that is, by exercising the "Philosophy of the Bomb".[59] They simply want to destroy cultures by disrupting peace and security. The detonation of a bomb represents the ultimate ambush; it catches people completely off guard, generates terror at the speed of the expanding gases, and increases the "emotional distance"

---

[58] Ibid., *xiv*.
[59] Walter Laqueur, *The Age of Terrorism* (Boston: Little, Brown, and Company, 1987), 48-51.

between the perpetrator and the innocent civilians they often kill.[60]

Bombs can be made so simple that a "child" could use them or they can represent super-sophisticated devices such as the Lake Tahoe Casino bomb that contained over 1,000 pounds of high-explosives, 34 switches, alternative detonators, and *could not* be defused.[61] Either way, the possibilities for expanding mayhem are infinite – merely matching the sophistication of the device with the training of the individual. For their role, socialists are usually more concerned about such issues as class struggles and worker's rights.[62] Their heyday appears to have been the late 1800s and early 1900s before unionism became a standard, if somewhat archaic, fixture in the global economy. Groups such as the Molly Maguires and the Western Union of Mineworkers freely practiced "working-class terrorism" to further their aims.[63]

The rise of free trade, right-to-work capitalism, and more disciplined unions have largely capped the extreme violence of one hundred years ago though, as in many aspects of modern life, these problems merely shifted towards the southern hemisphere.

The Argentine Model

What began with Fidel Castro and Ernesto "Che" Guevara in Cuba found itself transplanted in Argentina during the latter 1960s. Whereas the originators of this escalation could

---

[60] Grossman, *Defeating the Enemy's Will*, 167-169.
[61] U.S. Government, *Federal Bomb Intelligence: U.S. Government Guide to Terrorist Explosives* (Boulder: Paladin Press, 1991), 73-74.
[62] Laqueur, *Age of Terrorism*, 52-53.
[63] Ibid., 15.

rightly lay claim to the "Cuban Model", I have chosen to include Argentina for the precise period between 1969 and 1979 remained unlike any other period in global history, save for perhaps the gangsterism widespread throughout Chicago and the American Midwest during the 1920s.[64]

For a country that once quipped that "more people were hurt at a Mexican wedding than in an Argentine coup d'état", the 1970s ushered in a cruel reality that the people were not in Kansas anymore.[65] The nation had dealt with both Perons, which exhibited both leftist and rightist extremes, and a sizeable portion of their population felt that they represented the old guard for the Old World; yet what eventually happened to their country shattered these misconceptions.[66]

What *did* happen and what makes the Argentine Model so singularly represented here is that terrorism took to their country from both sides; from the agitators and the reactionaries. The leftist guerrillas sought to overthrow the establishment and the establishment worked aggressively to 'disappear' anyone and everyone who threatened security. Soon, the Spanish word *desaparecido* simply became a more "tasteful euphemism" for having had died under the auspices of the brutal government.[67]

Thus, when people simply "disappear" instead of die, it remains difficult to get a handle on the true level of terrorism that existed during this period within that nation, but the implications speak loudly nevertheless. The overreaction

---

[64] Robert Cox, "Total Terrorism: Argentina, 1969 to 1979" in *Terrorism, Legitimacy, and Power: The Consequences of Political Violence* ed. Martha Crenshaw (Middletown, CT: Wesleyan University Press, 1983), 124-142.
[65] Ibid., 129.
[66] Ibid.
[67] Ibid., 128.

towards the locals by the security forces ensured that the people delighted in the fact that many police officers and military personnel were, themselves, routinely assassinated.

Soon, the frenzy included journalists, priests, teachers, and nearly everyone else in otherwise prudent public life. For all their brutality, for the untold thousands of dead, for the existence of secret prisons run by both the military and police alike, there "was virtually no left-wing terrorist activity within Argentina" by 1980-1981.[68] Society had finally begun to tame the security forces, for the Argentines had fully believed that they were "the heirs to Western, Christian civilization" and had a most difficult time believing that their own security forces had become "more barbaric than the terrorists."[69]

What the Argentines had learned the hard way, was the instrument most useful in dealing with fanatical elements; a lesson plan which society had been dealing with for ages.

The Haqqani/al-Qaeda Model

By anyone's definition, this section could be adequately termed "The Islamist Model" and whether Shia or Sunni in origin, the implications remain the same. However, the distinction of the Jalaluddin Haqqani Network bears close scrutiny, for this remains the network that fostered Osama Bin Laden's al-Qaeda and fuels jihadist activities far beyond its Afghan base of operations. Emerging from an Afghan and Pakistani insurgency group during the 1970s, the Haqqani Network (HQN) shaped al-Qaeda's trajectory throughout the

---

[68] Ibid., 131.
[69] Ibid., 129.

region.[70]

Jalaluddin, during the Soviet invasion of Afghanistan, captured Khost and remained instrumental in placing together "a diverse constituency of groups" between Afghanistan and Pakistan.[71]Later on, during the 1980s, "Jalaluddin quickly rose to be one of the [Pakistani Intelligence Agency's] most favored field commanders."[72] More recently, the HQN serves as the Taliban's "force multiplier" strengthening the Islamist group's campaigns throughout the region.[73]

The connection between Haqqani, Bin Laden, the Taliban, Afghanistan, Pakistan, and Sudan underscores the fundamental support that HQN has provided al-Qaeda and, in fact, the Bin Laden group owes its very existence to Jalaluddin.[74]Nevertheless, al-Qaeda bears some unique differences that warrant discussion, despite the underlying support (and guidance) of HQN. Think of al-Qaeda – and its various post-9/11 supporters – as mere proxies of Jalaluddin and HQN.

Al-Qaeda's master plan represents a three-pronged attack against the West. These three phases of their "guerrilla war" are as follows:[75]

---

[70] Don Rassler and Vahid Brown, *The Haqqani Nexus and the Evolution of al-Qa'ida* (West Point, NY: Harmony Program, Combating Terrorism Center, U.S. Military Academy, July 14, 2011), 1.

[71] Ibid., 9-10.

[72] Ibid., 13.

[73] Ibid.

[74] Ibid., 30.

[75] Norman Cigar, trans. *Al-Qa'ida's Doctrine for Insurgency: 'Abd Al-'Aziz Al-Muqrin's A Practical Course for Guerrilla War* (Washington: Potomac Books, 2009), 92-102.

1. **Phase One: Attrition**. During this phase, the jihadists plan to 'hit and run' against their targets, allowing spectacular strikes in order to gain attention from the media and generate increase in recruiting efforts. Examples include 9/11, which drove a rift between the U.S. and Saudi Arabia, the attack upon the U.S.S. Cole and, undoubtedly, the recent attacks in Benghazi on September 11, 2012;

2. **Phase Two: Relative Strategic Balance**. During this phase, the jihadists seek an equilibrium that will permit them to set up base camps, hospitals, *Shari'a* courts, broadcasting stations, etc. within newly conquered, or in their terms, "liberated", locations. This possibly represents what has transpired throughout the Middle East/Northern Africa (MENA) following the so-called Arab Spring uprisings;

3. **Phase Three: Military Decision**. During this phase, the jihadists basically announce their 'arrival' within smaller cities and the countryside where they will shift their base camps and receive support from the broader Islamic community. Specifically, the jihadists plan to "intimidate" their enemies by stressing the inevitability of their surrender, during which *Shari'a* courts will be established to 'try' everyone who had rebelled against Islam.

Without a doubt, the Islamist game plan can be witnessed throughout the world today, as they secretly move into virgin territory, force the indigenous agencies to "overreact", thereby applying the "victimization" card all the while waiting for an opportunity to emerge victorious and convict those who tried to stop them. A sizeable portion of this effort, it would appear, utilizes the concept of *al-Taqiyya*, or deceit in order to blend in or deflect charges of subversion and hostility.

The Religious Model

Local populations swelled with those seeking disorientating rapid change. They felt that their rights had been eroded and that justice was not on their side, so they became frustrated with what they perceived to be authoritarian regimes that did not preserve local traditions based exclusively upon God's Law as outlined within bona fide religious texts. The Middle East today? No, German-speaking Europe during the 16th century.[76]

Religion today has become a blasé subject for some and an outright taboo for others. It comes therefore, as no surprise that most are fully disconnected with the intimate role that religion plays within global civilization. We have come to accept that "freedom of religion" means, specifically, that we are free *not* to have to deal with the subject rather than the more traditional interpretation that we are allowed to either choose our religious beliefs or choose not to accept any religious beliefs. This fine line between choosing not to practice religion and empowering us to deny religion completely remains a significant flaw within modern society.

With 92% of the world's population believing in theism and 84% subscribing to some form of institutionalized belief, it remains decidedly difficult to understand how some people can still conduct their lives without acknowledging that the

---

[76] Ralph Peters, "Rebels and Religion: How Fighters become Fanatics" *Armed Forces Journal* (January, 2007), 29.

rest of the planet remains overwhelmingly spiritual in nature.[77] This has grave consequences in regards to the study of terrorism and its current practitioners.

Faith today, especially within the Christian West, leaves much to be desired. Our forefathers *lived* for the afterlife; today we tend to fabricate terrestrial religiosity.[78]Religion has become a *mere part* of our lives, along with football, tractor pulls, dance music, and shuffling the kids off to grandma and grandpa so that we can enjoy a break from parental responsibilities. Religion used to *be* everyone's life – in Europe and elsewhere – but we contemporaries tend to mock those who exhibit even some of these traditional values.

Religion – of whatever flavor – enables the *true* believer to undertake the most extraordinary tasks. It represents what makes a mortal man, such as the aforementioned Simeon Stylites, live upon a stone pillar for most of his life and it is what makes impressionable teenagers strap on a bomb vest and detonate it within a crowd of wedding guests. It also defines the raw hatred of a Klan member and the selfless love of a soldier who throws his body upon a live grenade. 'It' is *all* about faith and how the individual person *perceives* this particular faith.

Religion is not simply about *believing in God*. Tens of millions of Americans alone "believe in God", but the relationship usually ends as soon as the statement leaves his or her lips. For example, there are probably some 80 million "Roman Catholics" within the United States today, but

---

[77] According to www.adherents.com, roughly one-half of the 16% "non-religious" people still believe within a divinity. The rest comprise atheists, agnostics, and others.
[78] Kreeft, *Everything you ever wanted to know*, 193

few, if any, strongly subscribe to Vatican doctrine. As soon as you hear, for instance, a politician spout affiliation with the Church *and* acceptance of the "right" for an individual to choose an abortion, then you have a misrepresentation of faith from that individual. The Church requires that the *"disciple of Christ must not only keep the faith and live it, but also profess it, confidently bear witness to it, and spread it: 'All however must be prepared to confess Christ before men and to follow him along the way of the Cross, amidst the persecutions which the Church never lacks.'"*[79] This includes politicians who are required to use their profession to spread the Gospels to all men.

Nevertheless, in truth, "it often remains the *minority* which remains faithful to a particular ideology or religion."[80] This thesis works two ways. One, the vast majority of Catholics within the United States who support, say, abortion, gay marriages, married priests, etc. are in error of the Church's 20-century-long established doctrine. On the other hand, the "silent majority" of the Muslim world know "very little about the teachings in the Quran and sunnah that give Muslims the right to use terrorist activity as a war method against the enemies of Islam."[81] There is little confusion, therefore, that the vast majority of Muslims act much as do the vast majority of Roman Catholics; both remain secularists at heart and understand very little about their faith's official doctrine.

Where problems occur, rests with the vast gap between the beliefs of devout Catholics and devout Islamists. No self-respecting Catholic (or even Protestant) would endorse

---

[79] *Catechism*, #1816.

[80] Godlewski, "Latte Intelligence", 77.

[81] Mark A. Gabriel, *Journey into the Mind of an Islamic Terrorist: Why they hate us and how we can change their minds* (Lake Mary, FL: FrontLine, 2006), 183

indiscriminate violence as a means of entering Heaven. In fact, the earliest Christians willingly went to the lions or burned alive as garden torches rather than offer harm towards another living soul. If we are, therefore, incapable of understanding a religion that has been part of our civilization for two thousand years, how much *more* incapable are we of understanding religions that are new (or, at a minimum, new to our nations)?

Religious terrorism represents far more than just Muslim extremists. For example, "historians report that there is a tradition of violence among the Sikhs."[82] The Thugs subscribed to a devotion to the goddess Kali.[83] Rarity does not preclude the potential and even mainstream religions, such as Hinduism, Buddhism, as well as Christianity bear the potential for misuse by individuals or cults. Today, faiths of which we may not even consider as "religious" in nature, such as environmentalism, progressivism, etc. fuel hatred and destruction amongst some adherents. The qualifier remains whether or not the devotee believes in his or her cause as *greater* than legitimate public law instituted by a free and unhampered electorate.

The Narco Model

In fullest disclosure, this represents less of a model than as an entire way of life. Narcotics cartels employ terrorism as simply a tool, one of many they employ against those who seek to stop them and against *all* competition. Nevertheless, no group of individuals bear more violence upon innocent souls than the narco-cartels populating Latin American and elsewhere. For our purposes, we need to address several

---

[82] Laqueur, *Age of Terrorism*, 233.
[83] Ibid., 13-14.

key factors. First, the most notorious narco-paramilitary group remains *Los Zetas*, an infamously deadly group founded by 31 deserters from Mexico's Airborne Special Forces Groups and originally aligned with the Gulf Cartel.[84]According to the U.S., *Los Zetas* represents the most violent, sophisticated, and threatening private army in Mexico.[85]

Already, such cartels – and the armies they employ – have warned U.S. agencies that the groups' snipers will target any off-duty (or sans uniform on-duty, apparently) law enforcement officers who attempt to thwart the drug trade, *even if those officers are in, say, Arizona.*[86]Besides the obvious, any narco-induced collapse of the Mexican economy threatens to turn the border region into a form of "Waziristan, U.S.A." as millions of potential immigrants flee northward to avoid the turmoil.[87]

The Lone Wolf Model

Some individuals just want to kill and/or maim as many of us as they can for an infinite number of perceived grievances. On May 18th, 1927 Andrew P. Kehoe drove his truck loaded with dynamite and rusty machinery parts to a Bath, Michigan school on the outskirts of Lansing and killed 38 children and 6 adults, including having had bludgeoned his wife back at his ranch.[88] His grievance? He was upset at

---

[84] Hal Brands, *Mexico's Narco-Insurgency and U.S. Counterdrug Policy* (Carlisle, PA: Strategic Studies Institute, May 2009), 8.
[85] Ibid.
[86] Mark Spicer, "Mexican Drug Cartels: The Growing Threat of the Sniper Attack", *Journal of Counterterrorism & Homeland Security International* 16, no. 4 (2011): 50.
[87] Kan, *"Narco-Refugees"*, 25-29.
[88]http://freepages.history.rootsweb.ancestry.com/~bauerle/disaster.htm. Accessed October, 2012.

the taxes levied upon him in order to pay for the tiny hamlet's school.[89] It *still* ranks as the worst school massacre in U.S. history. Theodore "Unabomber" Kaczynski and Eric Rudolph of the Olympic Park bombing both evaded arrest for years while they plied their murderous trade.

Making matters worse, lone wolf terrorists such as the "alleged" shooter down at Fort Hood, Texas, Nidal Hasan, may or may not be acting alone. Even the 1995 Oklahoma City bombing undertaken by Timothy McVeigh and Terry Nichols bears credulous influence from 1993 World Trade Center terrorist Ramzi Yousef.[90] That Nichols and Yousef ended up in Cebu City, Philippines during the same time and the OKC bomb design resting remarkably similar to the WTC bomb remains far more than interesting coincidence.[91] Remember, in nature, even lone wolves emerge from packs.

---

[89] Ibid.
[90] Peter Lance, *1000 Years for Revenge: International Terrorism and the FBI: The Untold Story* (New York: ReganBooks, 2003), 308-318.
[91] Ibid.

7 KNOW THYSELF.

Never had I become such a controversial figure than when I had begun to preach the need for individual involvement within the fight against terrorism. My steadfast opposition towards *all forms* of abortion seems to have generated little concern. My pro-American stance has created few enemies amongst my foreign readers. My overtly religious novels had caught very little attention, even from those who dismiss God. Even my openly Roman Catholic evangelization simply amuses my Protestant and Muslim friends.

However, as soon as I announced that fighting terrorism remains *everyone's business*, I became something of a renegade within society. Why? Undoubtedly, because whenever you mention fighting terrorism, one of only three thoughts immediately come to the mind of most individuals:

1. Combating terrorism remains the sole domain of Hollywood action flicks detailing the infamous (or fantastical) exploits of Navy SEALs, Delta Force, or some sinister CIA-based group;

2. Combating terrorism remains a police function to be handled *solely* by certified police officers, federal agents, or teams of international diplomats;

3. Terrorism is merely a minor disturbance that does not deserve the attention that it receives.

It is, and *always* has been (since at least ~1981), my personal belief that *everyone* must be involved within our national security, regardless of our profession or training. This is not an easy subject to consider, but just as the world's Muslims could not believe that nineteen Arab men could "fool the CIA" in order to pull off the September 11, 2001 attacks, we cannot do the opposite and rely *exclusively* upon our government or our military to protect us.[92] As ex-CIA operative, Robert Baer, wrote: "And what had saved the city I was living in? Not the CIA. Not the FBI. Not the air force or navy or marines or army. But the raw courage and determination of a fistful of average Americans."[93] The passengers of United Airlines Flight 93, in my estimation, represent the truest embodiment of independent counterterrorism.

Ignorance of events, whether from Arabs or Americans, is most definitely *not* a good thing. Why, therefore, are we predisposed to being "shocked" when horrible things happen? Why are we, as a nation, so incapable of protecting ourselves without relying upon our taxpayer-financed services? Because the fear of aggression has become our "mother's milk".[94] We simply are not reared to become *warriors* anymore. That we might actually be *bred* to fight is

---

[92] Gerges, *Journey of the Jihadist*, 183.
[93] Robert Baer, *See No Evil: The True Story of a Ground Soldier in the CIA's War on Terrorism* (New York: Three Rivers Press, 2002), 268.
[94] Balor, *Mercenary Solider*, 102.

never considered amongst even our "danger loving society."[95]We are simply so appalled at our fellow man's desire to terminate us that most of our species would willingly go to our deaths than to raise a single hand in defense of our own lives. Do not believe me? Remember, what is the *first* thing that a police officer or public official will tell you to do during a robbery or burglary? "Give them what they ask for. Your life is worth more than mere material possessions." Ever notice the news lately? Have you ever considered what would have happened if *all* aircraft passengers on 9/11 had fought back?

There remains many instances – just pay attention to the news – where some spunky gas station attendant or retailer thwarted a robbery, even against armed assailants, by fighting back. These do not represent isolated incidents, either. The main reason that the police tells you to give up is because they do not want to be sued by saying that, in many cases, merely giving up your prized possessions will *not* save your life. People rob you because they *believe* that they can get away with it. Ever notice the drop in crime for communities with concealed-carry permits? If you are afraid to die, then chances are so is the thug trying to rob you blind.

On September 11, 2001 Osama Bin Laden and his al-Qaeda organization did not believe for a moment that the United States would respond in the way that it did.[96]We did respond, however. Only 75% of the planes diverted to strike us on that infamous day succeeded in reaching their target; the fourth plane's passengers *fought back* Everyone aboard United Flight 93 knew they were going to die, but they chose

---

[95] Grossman, "Defeating the Enemy's Will", 151-153.
[96] Gerges, *Journey of the Jihadist*, 202-211.

to fight back in order to save their fellow citizens from a fate far worse than death. Of what great debt do we now owe them?

By not taking a stand – a realistic and actionable one, that is – against terrorism you have become your own worst enemy, which is why I have chosen to write a complete chapter on knowing *yourself*. It is when we, the common folk of this planet, determine that our lives are only worth as much as whatever someone *else* decides that it is worth do we allow ourselves to become truly worthless. Part of the reason is that we fear placing this life on the line. The rest of it is undoubtedly because we are afraid of placing our *rights* on the line. I, for one, have chosen to end this interminable dance with fate. *My* life is worth defending and worth defending, possibly, to the death. What say you?

Know Thy Territory

To simply know *who* is trying to kill you is definitely not enough. You must fully understand the geography of terrorism as well; and this, friend, means pretty much the entire planet. Chances are, however, that you get lost on your way to the local supermarket. Fortunately, unlike the terrorists themselves, knowing the planet, the nations that surround it, and the overall texture of the humanity that contaminates its surface, is a fairly straightforward process. I say this because physical and political structures do not evolve nearly as fast as the human minds that conceive of them.

You therefore possess more time in which to analyze Geospatial Intelligence – the combination of using computer software and analytical methods with terrestrial or geographic datasets – but, at this stage, you need not be so advanced in your activities.

What you need to do, for the moment, remains to concentrate on nations and their subcultures. You need to understand things such as national leadership, ethnic groups, religions, key industries, principal alliances, etc. The following comes from the U.S. Army's *Guerrilla Warfare and Special Forces Operations FM 31-21* field manual (9/1961). Using core data retrieved from the CIA's *World Factbook,* you can adapt these recommendations pursuant to your files on each nation:

General Area Study

General

1. Political

- Government, international political orientation, and degree of popular support;
- Attitudes of identifiable segments of the population toward the United States, its allies and the enemy;
- National historical background;
- Foreign dependence and/or alliances;
- National capitol and significant political, military and economic concentrations.

2. Geographic Positions

- Areas and dimensions;
- Latitude and climate;
- Generalized physiographic;

- Generalized land utilization;
- Strategic location:
    *Neighboring countries and borders;
    *Natural defenses including frontiers;
    *Points of entry and strategic routes;

3. Population

- Total and density;
- Breakdown into significant ethnic and religious groups;
- Division between urban, rural, and/or nomadic groups:
    *Large cities and
  population centers;
    *Rural settlement patterns;
    *Areas and movement
  patters of
    nomads.

4. National Economy

- Technological standards;
- Natural resources and degree of self-sufficiency;
- Financial structure and dependence upon foreign aid;
- Agriculture and domestic food supply;
- Industry and level of production;
- Manufacture and demand for consumer goods;
- Foreign and domestic trade and facilities;
- Fuels and power;
- Telecommunications and radio systems;
- Transportation – U.S. standards and adequacy:
    *Railroads;
    *Highways;

*Waterways;
Commercial air installations.

5. National Security

- Center of political power and the organization for national defense;
- Military forces (Air, Navy, Air Force); summary of order of battle;
- Internal security forces – summary of organization and strength;
- Paramilitary forces: summary of organization and strength.

Geography

- Climate. General classification of country as a whole with normal temperatures, rainfall, etc., and average seasonal variations;
- Terrain. General classification of the country noting outstanding features, i.e., coasts, plains, deserts, mountains, hills and plateaus, rivers, lakes, etc.
- Major Geographic Subdivisions. Divide the country into its various definable subdivisions each with generally predominant topographical characteristics, i.e., coastal plains mountainous plateau, rolling, heavily forested hills, etc. For each subdivision use the following outline in a more specific analysis of the basic geography:
  1. Temperature. Variations from normal and, noting the months in which they may occur, any extremes that would affect operations;

2. Rainfall and snow. Same as above;

3. Wind and Visibility. Same as above;

4. Relief:

*General direction of mountain ranges or ridge lines and whether hills and ridges are dissected;

*General degree of slope;

*Characteristics of valleys and plains;

*Natural routes for and natural obstacles to cross-country movement;

5. Land utilization. Not any peculiarities, especially the following:

*Former heavily forested areas subjected to widespread cutting or dissected by paths and roads; also, the reverse, i.e., pasture or waste land which has been reforested;

*Former waste or pasture land that has been resettled and cultivated – now being farmed or the reverse (former rural countryside that has been depopulated and allowed to return to waste land);

*Former swamp or marsh land that has been drained; former desert or waste land now irrigated and cultivated; and lakes created by dams;

6. Drainage. General pattern:

* Main rivers, direction of flow;

*Characteristics of rivers and streams such as current, banks, depths, type of bottom and obstacles, etc.

     *Seasonal variation, such as dry beds and flash floods;

     Large lakes or areas of many ponds and/or swamps.

7. Coast. Examine primarily for infiltration, exfiltration, and resupply points:

     *Tides and waves; winds and current;

     *Beach footing and covered exit routes;

     *quite coves and shallow inlets or estuaries;

8. Geological basics. Type of soil and rock formations (include areas for potential landing zones for small aircraft).

9. Forests and Other Vegetation. Natural or cultivated.

     *Type, characteristics and significant variations from the norm and at the different elevations;

     *Cover or concealment-density, seasonal variation;

10. Water. Ground, surface, seasonal and potable;

11. Subsistence. Noting whether seasonal or year-round:

     *Cultivated – vegetables, grains, fruits, nuts, etc.

     *Natural – berries, fruits, nuts, herbs, etc.

     *Wildlife – animals, fish, and fowl.

People

The following sub-outline should be used for an analysis of the population in any given region or country or as the basis for an examination of the people within a subdivision as suggested above. In all events particular attention should be given to those areas within a country where the local inhabitants have peculiarities and are at considerable variance in one or more ways from the normal, national way of life.

- Basic Racial Stock and Physical Characteristics. (1) Types, features, dress, and habits. (2) Significant variations from the norm;
- Standard of Living and Cultural (Education) Levels. (1) Primarily note the extremes away from average. (2) Class structure (Degree of established social stratification and percentage of population in each class);
- Health and Medical Standards. (1) Common Diseases. (2) Standards of Public Health. (3) Medical Facilities and Personnel. (4) Potable water supply. (5) Sufficiency of medical supplies and equipment;
- Ethnic Components. This should be analyzed only if of sufficient size, strength and established bonds to constitute a dissident minority of some consequence. (1) Location or concentration. (2) Basis for discontent and motivation for change. (3) Opposition to majority and/or to the political regime. (4) Any external or foreign ties of significance;
- Religion. (1) Note wherein the national religion definitely shapes the actions and attitudes of the individual. (2) Religious divisions. Major and minor religious groups of consequence;
- Traditions and customs (Particularly taboos.) Note wherever they are sufficiently strong and

established that they may influence an individual's actions or attitude even during a war situation;

- Rural countryside. (1) Peculiar or different customs, dress and habits. (2) Village and farm buildings – construction materials;
- Political Parties or Factions. (1) If formed around individual leaders or based on established organizations. (2) If a single dominant party exists, is it nationalistic in origin or does it have foreign ties? (3) Major legal parties with their policies and goals. (4) Illegal or underground parties and their motivation. (5) Violent opposition factions within major political organizations;
- Dissidence. General active or passive potential, noting if dissidence is localized or related to external movements;
- Resistance (Identified movements). Areas and nature of activities, strength, motivation, leadership, reliability, possible contacts and external direction or support;
- Guerrilla groups. Areas and nature of operations, strength, equipment, leaders reliability, contacts and external direction or support.

Enemy

- Political. (1) Outside power (Number and status of non-national personnel, their influence, organization and mechanism of control). (2) Dominant National Party. Dependence upon and ties with an outside power; strength, organization, and apparatus; evidences of dissension at any level in the party; and the location of those areas within the country that are under and especially strong or weak non-national control;

- Conventional Military Forces (Army, Navy, Air Force).

(1) Non-national or occupying forces in the country:

(a) Morale, discipline, and political reliability;

(b) Personnel strength;

(c) Organization and basic development;

(d) Uniforms and unit designations;

(e) Ordinary and special insignia;

(f) Leadership (officer corps);

(g) Training and doctrine;

(h) Equipment and facilities;

(i) Logistics;

(j) Effectiveness (any unusual capabilities or weaknesses).

(2) National (indigenous) forces (Army, Navy, Air Force) and repeat (a) through (j) above;

- Internal Security Forces (including border guards).

(1) Strength and general organization, distinguishing between non-national and national elements:

(a) Overall control mechanism;

(b) Special units and distinguishing insignia;

(c) Morale, discipline and relative loyalty of native personnel to the occupying or national regime;

(d) Non-national surveillance and control over indigenous security forces;

(e) Vulnerabilities in the internal security system;

(2) Deployment and disposition of security elements:
    (a) Exact location down to the smallest unit or post;
    (b) Chain of command and communication;
    (c) Equipment, transportation and degree of mobility;
    (d) Tactics (seasonal and terrain variations);
    (e) Methods of patrol, supply and reinforcements;

(3) The location of all known guard posts or expected wartime security coverage for all types of installations, particularly along main LOCs (railroads, highways, and telecommunications lines) and POL lines;

(4) Exact location and description of the physical arrangement and particularly of the security arrangements of all forced labor or concentration camps and any potential POW enclosures;

(5) All possible details, preferably by localities, of the types and effectiveness of internal security controls, including checkpoints, identification cards, passports and travel permits.

Targets

The objective in target selection is to inflict maximum damage on the enemy with minimum expenditure of men and material. Initially, the operational capabilities of a guerrilla force [AUTHOR'S NOTE: Translate into counterterrorism force] may be limited in the interdiction or destruction of enemy targets. The target area and the specific points of attack must be studied, carefully planned and priorities established. In general, targets are listed in order of   priority:

- Railroads. (1) Considerations in the selection of a particular line – (a) importance, both locally and generally; (b) bypass possibilities; (c) number of tracks and electrification. (2) Location of maintenance crews, reserve repair facilities and equipment. (3) Type of signal and switch equipment. (4) Vulnerable points – (a) unguarded small bridges or culverts; (b) cuts, fills, overhanging cliffs or undercutting streams; (c) key junctions or switching points; (d) tunnels. (5) Security systems.

- Telecommunications.
- POL.
- Electric Power.
- Military Storage and Supply.
- Military Headquarters and Installations.
- Radar and Electronic Devices.
- Highways.
- Inland Waterways/Canals.
- Seaports.
- Natural and synthetic gas lines.
- Industrial plants.

At this point, you are probably overwhelmed over the amount of information that the foregoing *General Area Study* requires. Not to worry, the vast majority of it will not apply to you. However, I have included it for several reasons, all of which I consider important to your role of *active* counterterrorist. First, this remains a lifelong pursuit that your are undertaking and as the world and your adversaries evolve, you are going to have to develop your own intelligence database of existing and potential threats to your nation and, most especially, to our way of life (particularly if you do a great deal of overseas travel).

Secondly, the advent of the Internet and high-speed data communications provide you with the *opportunity* to establish a rudimentary intelligence *network* that represents a fundamental need in tracking and eliminating terrorist threats – so what was once required of a complete battalion to undertake can now be achieved by small groups or individuals who consciously set aside the time and initiative to track down some of this information. Finally, just because *you* have not determined a need for collecting this information regarding, say, Iran, Pakistan, ,or Somalia, do not believe for a moment that your terrorist enemies are not collecting such information about you or your own nation and its allies.

In fact, knowing *what* enemies might be seeking of your own nation falls under the discipline of *counterintelligence* and your efforts may be most helpful to your own federal and military forces – which is why *you* are getting involved within counterterrorism activities in the first place. Therefore, for those of you who do a great deal of travel abroad, start educating yourself regarding the places that you tour and for those of you eternally planted within your own country, start seeking out those who wish to harm you there.

There is one subject more important than perhaps just knowing about the world's people and nations, however. The knowledge remains interconnected, but the effort is no less demanding or important. You have to understand the *languages* of this vast world of ours.

Talk the Talk

Unless you can communicate in a language other than your own, you remain at a distinct disadvantage when it comes to protecting your family and friends – not to mention your country and global security. Nationalistic appeal aside, there rests no legitimate reason to be singularly linguistic in today's day and age of globalization.

Whether the Polish I learned as a kid owing to my own heritage; the French that I studied rather poorly while in high school; the Japanese that I absorbed while deployed to Japan for three months; the Tagalog that assured some semblance of survival while visiting Subic Bay; the brief Korean picked up while stopping at Pusan; the Brazilian Portuguese studied for my trip to the Amazon; the Spanish required for jobs where I was the *only* one who spoke English; the Russian that I picked up at Michigan State, the Ukrainian of my good friend; or the Arabic that I have studied both academically and professionally; I have myself learned how quickly one can not only be required to deviate from their native tongue, but how easy it can be to learn enough of another language to survive. And I did not even bring up Farsi, Hebrew, and Amharic.

With the availability of technology today, anyone can begin to practice a new language of his or her choosing. You have, for instance, Rosetta Stone® software, videos appearing on YouTube, and even Defense Language Institute programs available for purchase via eBay. The conscientious citizen will be able to learn to read, write, and speak a new language with unheard of rapidity.

For combating terrorism, you need to become familiar with at least one of the following languages – Arabic, Farsi, Spanish or Russian, depending upon your location. With the way the world is going, I would also recommend the dialects surrounding Afghanistan and Pakistan, perhaps Central and Northern Africa as well. *Any* knowledge will further your cause to delve into tracking the beasts and keeping yourself alive during the process. Remember, however, that 99% of what you will undoubtedly be doing remains within your own backyard.

This is, after all, not an all-inclusive manual; it represents a guidebook to steer you into the right direction. A book designed to work with the free *Independent Counterterrorist* training modules which can be updated and tailored towards rising threats. Your fundamental desire upon completing this book remains to be able to formulate something of a warrior intent within your personality. It represents 'Boot Camp' of a sort and much training and personal conditioning lies ahead. Again, you *do not want* your adversaries understanding what you know. الآن ؟ ف همت هى

Walk the Walk

When handsome "youthful and ruddy" David pledged to fight 6'6" Goliath of Gath for King Saul, the king thought that the kid was absolutely nuts: "*You cannot go up against this Philistine and fight with him, for you are only a youth, while he has been a warrior from his youth.*"[97] Undeterred with this bit of generational prejudice, David simply replied: "*Your servant used to tend his father's sheep, and whenever a lion or bear came to carry off a sheep from the flock, I would go after it and attack it and rescue the prey from its mouth. If it attacked me, I would seize it by the jaw, strike it, and kill it.*"[98] So much for the timid little shepherd boy...

We *all* know how the story ended. David used his trusty sling to embed a stone into his opponent's forehead

---

[97] 1 Samuel 17:33, *NAB*
[98] Ibid., 34-35.

rendering the much larger individual dead – at least as dead as one could ascertain without a modern medical examiner present – and finished his adversary off with a beheading from Goliath's own sword (which effectively eliminated the need for any modern medical examiner). David went on to become king, chose whatever wife he wanted (even if she was already married at the time), and fathered a son whose eventual wealth and prosperity would make *any* parent damn proud of him.

There are several morals in this tale which apply directly to you. First, you do not need the best technology available in the world to defeat your enemy. You just need the most effective technology *available to you*. Secondly, you do not have to be as large or as massive as either your enemy or the forces too inept to fight them on their own accord. Finally, and this is by far the most important lesson, David knew how to ensure that his enemy was dead by decapitating the giant. We do not need to become *that* barbaric, but we must become that *thorough*. Just as with David, when we fight our enemies, we must ensure that they remain incapable of attacking us without the need for a licensed medical examiner to determine their status.

Far too often within our society, we try to *civilize* our response to threats and the only thing that we manage to do is to ensure that our enemies live again to fight another day. Consider former President Jimmy Carter who had reduced U.S. covert operations capabilities by 40% from 1977 to 1979 to avoid having the CIA conduct "dirty work."[99] Our embassy in Tehran (as well as the one in Pakistan) was stormed by Islamic "students" in 1979. Perfect timing.

---

[99] Stephen F. Knott, *Secret and Sanctioned: Covert Operations and the American Presidency* (New York: Oxford University Press, 1996), 174.

Carter's own national security advisor noted concerns over "the astonishing lack of information" following the Shah's collapse and the subsequent seizure of our sovereign territory.[100] The Islamic Republic of Iran and its tyrannical mullahs have been a thorn in our side ever since and the current liberal administration in Washington appears content to repeat these same errors. Makes you wonder how differently things would have been today if we had just gone ahead and bombed the Ayatollah back into the Stone Age, right?

Instead, we evolved into a nation where the U.S. Army spent $100 *Billion* developing its new Future Combat Systems (FCS) program, but showcased the technology within a lame, politically-correct video where one child was saved from a virus and five "clownish terrorists" were apprehended by we 'good guys'.[101] Nobody bothers to tell our government and our citizenry that "war means fighting and fighting means killing."[102] Our nation might be obsessed with "kindness" but if you use it as a platform on which to protect your family, you will end up on the losing end. Period.

Think of it what you may, but our national defense remains predicated upon transitory politics. What one administration may enforce today, another may deny tomorrow and vice versa. This means that the safety of your loved ones boils down to what is currently rising within the polls – unless *you* act. You must, I cannot state often enough, dedicate the *entirety of your life* to combating terrorism even if it has to be shared with your other

---

[100] Ibid., 175.
[101] Ralph Peters, "Killing with Kindness: Political Correctness Infiltrates the Army" *Armed Forces Journal* (December 2006), 28.
[102] Ibid., 30.

responsibilities. Inasmuch as one cannot expect to breathe *only* 85% of the time, one cannot contribute only one or two days per week or even "only" ten or twenty years to survival. It must represent an "all or nothing" proposition.

To formulate some strategic thinking within your day, I suggest patterning your life after the color code system developed by retired Colonel Jeff Cooper of the Marines:[103]

Color Code for Personal Awareness

- **White.** This represents the state of being "Fat, Dumb, and Happy". You are totally relaxed; completely unprepared for anything. You may be in this condition within your own home particularly if you own security systems, guard dogs, and even weapons. Attacked while in "white mode" and you probably will not survive one minute.

- **Yellow.** Here you are relaxed, but with a non-specific alert. No immediate threat exists, but you still remain alert eying all possibilities. No one can approach you without your being aware of them. You are not anticipating any trouble, mind you, but are nevertheless prepared for it. You are within this condition, say, whenever you drive your vehicle, checking your mirrors frequently looking for obstacles even though they may not be there and wearing your seatbelt even though you do not anticipate any collisions.

- **Orange.** This represents a specific alert status. *Something* – a person, a vehicle, a situation – grabbed your attention. There might be a very simple and innocent reason for your heightened concerns, but you just want to be on your guard before you shift back down into Condition Yellow.

- **Red.** This represents the "fight is on!" mode that you dread experiencing, but spent your entire life preparing for; the situation where your mental "go" button is pressed. Someone

---

[103] Erik Lawrence, *Tactical Pistol Shooting: Your Guide to Tactics That Work* (Iola, WI: Gun Digest Books, 2005), 14-16.

might be approaching you with a gun, a raised baseball bat, or wielding a knife. This is where your "kill or be killed" posture comes into play even if it might not be ultimately exercised. A simple "If you do 'X' then I will do 'Y' algorithm. You are not 100% positive as to what your adversary will do, but you sure as hell know what *you* will do should the threat warrant.

It goes without saying that you should never allow yourself to be caught "pants down" in Condition White. Even while sleeping, your conditioned, subconscious mind still functions; just make certain it understands what is "home" and what is "strange". Remember, "A simple plan, well-rehearsed and violently executed, offers the best chance for success."[104] I just love the *violently* executed phrase. It goes with what Napoleon once spoke of regarding the concept of speed: *"I may lose a battle, but I will never lose a minute."*

Thus far within this book, we have discussed the imperative to fight, the power of faith in combat and survival, the need for conditioning yourself both mentally and physically – even to the point of developing something of the "ancient ninja" within your life. We examined your learning habits and how to improve them, as well as a bit about your various terrorist enemies and their supporters. We discussed delving into knowing as much about the physical and social world around us and presented a case for learning a few of the languages of this world. Most importantly, we just finished discussing the need to "walk the walk" instead of merely stating that we wish to do something about protecting ourselves and our loved ones.

Ultimately, there may come a point within your life when all of the preventative measures in the world fail and you find

---

[104] Ibid., 17.

yourself confronted with the proverbial "do or die" situation. Herein, you will discover once and for all whether you possess what it takes to literally take another's life (or at least gravely wound them). I will not make any pretense about it; it remains a thought that scares even the most hardened of souls. What happens when that situation arises can only be determined by you. Armies have "fought" for centuries trying to figure out ways in which to make their soldiers fight for real, but the truth remains that only a very small handful of individuals actually see combat. It is not very different today than it was during the American Civil War when 27,574 muskets were recovered from the Gettysburg battlefield – 24,000 were loaded; 12,000 of these were loaded more than once; and 6,000 of the multiply-loaded firearms had from three to ten rounds jammed within the barrel (one weapon was even loaded 23 times without having been fired!).[105]

What this says about us is that we fear "looking weak" nearly as much as we fear fighting itself. We will load guns again and again without firing a single shot, but we will die at least looking as if we are fighting. Fortunately, technology has eliminated such redundancy, but only *you* can actually squeeze the trigger upon another human being. This is probably a question that you have asked yourself a million times in the past, especially whenever you have watched a Hollywood 'action' movie on television or in the theater.

Myself, I guess that I have never had this problem. I was about seven years old when I shot my older brother in the leg with a pellet gun. I was even younger when I drove a pencil deeply into his leg, leaving a gruesome blemish to this

---

[105] Grossman, "Defeating the Enemy's Will", 158.

very day. I have said it once and I have said it a thousand times since – I have never, *ever* injured another living soul that did not *deserve* it. ☺

8 ARMS OF THE TRADE.

When avoidance and patience have failed and the need arises for personal defense, you can count on an infinite variety of weapons available – both improvised and purchased – to aid in your particular situation. We shall discuss each category and implement my personal recommendations. Each one of you will have your own thoughts, your own budget to work with, and your own physical limitations. More importantly, this chapter inherently favors (and remains directed towards) American citizens who, by virtue of the U.S. Constitution, specifically the Second Amendment, possess the right to keep and bear arms. Therefore, as with *everything* about combating terrorism, you must study on your own, seek out further resources, and employ sound judgment and common sense.

My recommendations herein thus merely reflect what particular image I bear of an independent counterterrorism agent; your needs and requirements reflect upon your particular situation, motivation, desires, finances, and applicable laws. We all have our "dream list", even our "bucket list", as well as our "permissible list". As the world grows more dangerous and the rest of us slowly catch up to fact, our own laws may begin to reflect upon this need.

For example, at the time of this writing, the concealed-carry map remains fluid with most states providing some form of right-to-carry. Illinois remains the sole holdout and a handful represent "may issue" states, meaning that they want to ensure that you meet all of their requirements before they even consider handing out your carry permit. Three states, Arizona, Vermont, and Alaska, permit concealed carry *without* a permit Most states that issue permits recognize other states concealed carry permits, meaning that a resident of Michigan can drive all the way to Florida armed.[106]

Now that we have whetted your appetite for what remains to come, it is to our distinct advantage to begin our discussion of weapons with the most available of all – those that God has given you. There will come a time when, all the permits and rights in the world aside, you will find yourself within a critical situation where *no* weapons are available and you must defend yourself accordingly.

Unarmed Combat

We have already discussed your martial arts training; this section will be geared more towards *targeting*. Even if you should, God forbid, find yourself confronted face-to-face with an armed assailant, all is not lost – you *do* have options. While your body may not be made of stone and your hands

---

[106] This 2012 version of *Mini-Manual* dispenses with both the conceal-carry map and the list of state reciprocity laws as that information was dated from 2006. Where laws are considered, it remains best not to suggest them within print and recommend that the reader explore the pertinent laws of his or her state. For broader information, please visit sites such as http://www.usconcealedcarry.net.

quite delicate instruments of manipulation, the same holds true for your attacker. That he or she may possess a knife, a firearm, or even a broadsword does not in any way, shape, or form increase the strength of their vulnerable points.

Consider the following scenario:

> A man stops you leaving your ATM machine at midnight, leveling a 9mm automatic at you midsection with his right hand and demands the cash that you just withdrew from the machine. What *do* you do?

Most people would probably collapse to the ground, losing their money in the process. A few others might go catatonic, fumbling around hysterically for the money that they already possess within their hands. At best, all of the above would be hoping, subconsciously, that someone *else* would be courteous enough to place a phone call to the community's *post event* responders.[107] Remember, it is the police and the politicians who have told you to capitulate and then *wait* for the appropriate authorities to arrive. They say this because they know full well that when *you* need them, they are most likely serving someone *else* many miles away.

In fact, in a ~2008 shooting in Detroit where a little seven-year-old handicapped girl was shot *several* times protecting her mother, it took *three calls to 911 before the police eventually showed up!* The first call was disconnected; the second call merely led to the emergency operator telling the caller that there were no units in the area to respond – *remember that line folks, remember it well* – and the third call, which finally got some reaction out of Detroit's finest, had to be placed by the gas station attendant himself. Besides the sheer bravery of that little girl – now there *is*

---

[107] Lawrence, *Tactical*, 10.

someone who would make a great counterterrorist! – this story shows that help, even within a major U.S. city, is never, *ever* going to respond to your expectations.

So what *might* you do in the situation outside your ATM machine? For starters, how about:

> In a *split-second* you strike his right wrist with your right hand pushing his arm towards your left, holding his wrist firm within your grip. Immediately, you use your left hand to bend the gun backwards – employing the pivot point of his wrist which you are currently holding – taking it away from him or knocking it towards the ground. *Simultaneously*, you deliver a *powerful* kick to his groin disabling the attacker.[108]If he does not cease and desist after you have acquired his gun, you might consider shooting the creep between the eyes, but I do not want you to turn bloodthirsty on me. That is definite *not* what this book is all about. However, if you are still agitated and fumbling with the phone, give him one more sound kick to the groin. That will make you feel a little better and keep him from running away.

This may not have been amongst your first thoughts, but it should have been amongst your first options. **Unnecessary delay in action may result in the loss of your life.** Did you, for example, actually believe that the thug would not have killed you after you would have given him your money? Times are changing; people are becoming more vicious and no decent hoodlum wants a witness around who can identify him. Will the above action work for *you*? Impossible to tell, but that is not the point. I have merely outlined a *possible response* where, perhaps, thirty seconds ago you possessed none. I have merely outlined one possible response to one

---

[108] Steve Crawford, *Deadly Fighting Skills of the World* (London: Brown Books, 1997), 14-15.

possible threat scenario in order to present the case that you *do* possess options, even when confronting the worst possible situations.

More likely than not, the creep with the gun did not expect you to do anything other than what *he* wanted you to do. There is, after all, no longevity in robbing people known or expected to be armed themselves. Consider, Goliath; he did not expect tiny little David to unleash a rock upside his head. As powerful as he was; as terrible as his reputation was; as sharp as his sword was, big bad Goliath was felled by one well-placed shot from a young rock slinger – something of a forerunner to today's professional snipers, to be sure.

There remains another, perhaps less enjoyable, thought for you to consider within the foregoing ATM scenario. Your body has only a few extremely vital target spots – we will discuss wound ballistics in a bit – and even at close range, you present a very small target. Forcing the robber's gun away, even by a small degree, removes his line of firing away from your most vulnerable midsection. Even if he were to pull the trigger, the more that you can deflect his gun away from you, the better for your chances of survival. I, for one, would rather take a shot in the arm than one into the gut.

Whatever the situation, there remains one key factor to be discussed. While the gunman may not be expecting you to fight back, *you*, on the other hand, must be prepared to do *something* to restore the situation back into your control. This means practice, training, forethought, and dedication to your life. Your rapid *actions* – not hysterical reactions – undoubtedly will catch most criminals off guard. They simply expect average citizenry to capitulate and fork over their money and possessions. This means that events will turn into your favor while your opponent goes into *"Damn, I did not expect them to do that!"* mode. Time is the most precious commodity of all, which is why, during our discussion on martial arts, I warned you to stay away from reliance upon "sport" techniques that merely indoctrinate you into fairness and civility.

Therefore, for example, should you ever successfully disarm a gun-carrying opponent and drop them down onto the ground, go ahead and stomp on their face a couple of times. It will teach them a lesson and you will walk away a bit calmer for the effort. Sure, the police will probably arrest you. Sure, the courts will probably try you. Sure, the bastard's own legal team will probably sue *you*. Nevertheless, were *they* around to help when needed? Probably not. Besides, ask for a trial by a jury of *your* peers. They probably hate the system as much as you do.

The reoccurring theme here is not to be brutal for its own sake. Contrary to popular opinion, I do not lead such a barbaric life myself. In all probability, I am one of the nicest individuals that you could ever met. I am intelligent, have a very spontaneous wit (that takes some time getting used to ☺), and possess a deep, rational concern for my fellow human beings. That said, I would like to provide you with two stories that bear strong parables. The first involves an episode while I was assigned to my third ship in the Navy, a destroyer. We were being repaired within the shipyard at that particular time and I, having just had the entirety of my large toenail removed, was serving 'light duty' aboard the barge that substituted for our electrical shop.

Four of us were in the shop on that day, my first class

petty officer, my second class petty officer, myself, and this huge brute that was eventually dishonorably discharged on cocaine possession or something. Anyway, this guy was about three sizes bigger than I was and decided that he wanted to thump his finger on my bad toe, delivering a shock of pain whenever he flicked the wounded appendage. At first, I did nothing because I erroneously concluded that my superiors, who were seated a very short distance away, would do something about it. By his fourth thump, I had had enough, supervisors present or not, I reached up and grabbed the jerk by the throat and threw him backwards over his stool.

The absolute glare within my eyes must have froze him because he did not move a muscle while I read him the riot act for about five minutes. After that day, my "Goliath" and all of his doper friends would not lift a finger to rile me. Lesson learned: I *will* defend myself, so even if I may appear docile, do *not* let my demeanor deceive you.

The second story involves my old dog, an Australian Cattle Dog, or Blue Heeler. He had a peculiar habit of covering his dog food dish with doilies, unwashed clothes, or anything else that he could find within reach. He even liked to bury his "business" atop a small bush or back up against a tree rather than defecate out in the open. Despite this, he had been known to drop a 2,000 pound bull who had become rather troublesome.

Several years ago, my dog had broken loose from the yard (he always had a bit of Houdini in him) and spent an all-nighter away from the house. His festivities ended when he was attacked by another dog and nearly died from the encounter. The veterinary assistant replied that he had undoubtedly learned his lesson and would no longer be a problem. The very next day, my dog snuck out again, probably to go after the sonofabitch (quite literally termed, I might add). I am the *same* way.

No, I do not like it whenever people glorify death and killing, but I am not afraid to defend myself either – even if, like my dog, it means finding myself lying near death on some farmer's field. Should I ever be attacked, I, too, will go after my adversaries for no other reason than to make them *pay* for their crimes. And I possess a *long-term* memory. This might mean legal restitution. It might mean armed encounters on the other side of the planet should they remain a threat to innocent bystanders. This is the way that it *has* to be when dealing with terrorists and transnational criminals. We have to keep pounding at them until *we* are safe enough to go back to living our quaint little lives *wherever* we choose to settle down.

As I have said, the human body remains a very frail instrument and this aids us when confronting threats unarmed. There remains several vulnerable spots to target:[109]

- Trachea, neck, larynx, neck arteries, neck veins, esophagus;

- Eyes, nose, mouth, chin, ears, jawbone, skull-spine juncture;

- Base of the skull, seventh vertebra, kidneys, renal artery and vein;

---

[109] Haha Lung, *Assassin! The Deadly Art of the Cult of the Assassins* (New York: Citadel Press, 1997), 107-121.

- Hips, stomach, thigh, calf, shin, top of foot, all joints and articulations;

- Rectum, groin.

Some of these areas work better with knives and other weapons, but do not underestimate the power of your hand once you have conditioned it through your physical-martial program. You will possess the option of applying the kick, the punch (or strike), place pressure or attempt strangulation, pull, bite, and use leverage against the joints and articulations. The *types* of injuries that we can instill upon our foes range from several pain or trauma (broken bone, kick in the groin, etc.) to knocking them out (punch in the chin, etc.) to even death (broken neck) – all with our bare hands and feet.

Perhaps the easiest targets for you to seek are: the groin (kicking, hitting, squeezing), the nose (fist punch, hammer blow), top of the foot (stomping), the shins (kicking), and the kidneys (karate blow, fist punch, kicking) all of which cause severe trauma within your opponent, though intense pressure on the testicles can lead to death. The two targets that can *permanently* incapacitate your attacker are the back of the neck (karate blow, hammer blow) and the clavicle hollow of neck (severe pressure, stabbing). To be effective, however, you must exercise and practice your punches, strikes, etc. to gain the strength needed for when the time should come. Fill up an old duffle bag with sand or heavy clothing, perhaps use an old chair as your punching bag. Just wrap your hands up so you do not suffer any injuries during practice and whale away on your target, concentrating on coordinated actions delivering beefy punches and kicks and not just wimpy throws of flesh.

Weapons of Opportunity

Rarely, if ever, will you find yourself in a position where there is *nothing* around that you can turn to your advantage. I have already mentioned how a spunky five-year-old can bring down his older brother with a pencil. Relax, he is fine. He grew up to be one of the top law enforcement officers in the country within his chosen specialty. We do not talk much today...

Anyway, the point remains – quite literally – that anything that does possess a nice, sharp point can be applied to devastating effect upon an individual. A pencil, a pen, an umbrella end, even a piece of stick can be used to pierce the human body.

What you need to do is make a habit of examining things around you that may come into play at any given moment. If you are attacked in a restaurant, do you throw coffee into the assailant's face and then follow up with the knife and fork to his eyes? Or do you need the knife and fork to buy time in order to reach the boiling pot of coffee?

While shopping, do you use your heavy shopping bag against his body or your purse (if you are a woman) upside his head followed by a swift kick to the groin? Outside in the parking lot, do you gouge his eyes out with your keys or do you have a sock loaded with coins that you can employ as a very lethal club? Perhaps you reside out West and have a big ol' buckle on your belt that you have learned to swing with all of the effort of a champion roper?

Truck drivers generally carry some form of billy to thump their tandem wheels in order to check for flat tires. Unfortunately, we were never allowed then to carry weapons and even our clubs were considered illegal if kept in the cab. However, many enterprising drivers kept short brooms in their cab that had – you guessed it – very stout handles that had a habit of loosening with ease. They simply improvised to suit their need. Myself, when I ran refrigerated trailers, I keep a long meat hook (borrowed from hauling swing beef) that I ostensibly used to pull my fifth wheel pin when dropping trailers off. In reality, it served as a weapon and with practice I found that I could take out a hand-sized chunk of wood from trees or two-by-fours with ease. Imagine its use upon a person.

You need to venture back into traditional semantics when being unarmed meant being *limbless*. You must constantly gaze about you and see things, not as utensils or commodities, but as potential weapons of opportunity. Do *not* terrify your wife or girlfriend during dinner by salivating over the thought of bashing your neighbor's brains out with the deep dish pizza pan. Just understand that the pizza pan is *there*, is fairly heavy, and easy to grasp (although probably *very hot*) and file that knowledge immediately away into your primed subconscious mind.

Improvised weapons – or weapons of opportunity as I like to call them – are just that; things that might aid in your survival situation should the need arise. Seek them out, but do not go overboard unless the situation warrants. Then, throw literally *everything* that you can at your target.

Edged Weapons

Knives can represent far more than just utility devices; they can be powerful instruments of destruction. Nevertheless, for all of their practicality and convenience, I do not recommend their use beyond, perhaps, keeping your hands and weapons of opportunity from being required. Fighting with knives represents something that just cannot be learned through a few weekend sessions as they are not "point and shoot" devices such as guns. And, God forbid, *do not even think about throwing knives* at your enemy. If you miss – and you probably will as moving targets are hard to hit even with firearms – then you have simply given your weapon to someone who, if he did not before, probably wants to kill you more than ever now.

For a knife to be used as a lethal instrument, the most proper technique applied is to simply thrust the blade into your opponent's most vulnerable spot as quickly and as frequently as possible. Ideally, this remains the kidneys which, incidentally, provides a much faster method of incapacitating a person than those quirky cover-the-mouth-and-slit-the-throat moves seen in war movies. Someone with a throat gouged out can *still* make a sound, but if a relatively tiny kidney stone can drop a full-grown man, just imagine what a Ka-Bar® could do thrust into one of his kidneys.

Forget fancy posturing moves pulled from movies such as *West Side Story*; once you realize that a grave threat exists, you should already be exercising that lovely tactic known affectionately as disemboweling your enemy. Knives and other edged weapons represent a last resort. A bit more practical than bare knuckles, perhaps, but not anything that should require your time and effort to the exclusion of firearms and avoidance. This said, I will offer a few pointers and leave the reader to investigate on his or her own.

When I drove within the household goods industry many years ago, I had once made a purchase of an awesome looking "survival knife" fashioned much like the one that became famous within the movie *First Blood*. Being required to move people into and out of some of America's most notorious cities, I felt decidedly more protected with its 12-inch blade hanging from my hip. Inside of the handle were matches, a fishing rig, a wire saw, and the cap itself contained a compass – important considerations to possess for all of those runs we made into Western and Northwestern states.

My knife was not cheap, but it was not handcrafted either. Not in the sense that some craftsman staked his livelihood and reputation on the quality leastways. The blade served its purpose as a deterrent well – people used to cross the street against traffic just to avoid walking near my truck when they saw it – and it sliced through boxes and packing tape efficiently. It was when I had to employ the knife within its "prying" mode that I realized just how cheesy the instrument truly was. The blade simply bent with the slightest ease. I suspect, now, that it would have bent even if it was lodged between a person's ribs. I do not mess with inferior quality "experimental" blades anymore and it remains nonsense to employ them as a *deterrent*.

I demand a knife that can be used to serve a range of needs – cut vines in the bush, skin a grizzly (and lower mammals), deflect an oncoming blade in close quarters battle should *that* need ever arise and, of course, penetrate an enemy's body easily and repeatedly. Naturally, some blades are better suited for some tasks than others, so I am forced to admit some degree of compromise. For instance, a Fairburn knife is good for stabbing and even slashing, but as an overall tool, it leaves much to be desired. Therefore, choose any form of "combat knife", with or without a serrated edge, and you should do okay.[110]

Brand names are numerous and I suggest that you concentrate on offerings from Ka-Bar®, Ontario Knife Company, and Cold Steel®. This also leads to a discussion on other forms of *edged* weapons. Some, writing for readers in locations where firearms remain prohibited, suggest a range of weapons from swords, to axes, and even machetes.[111]Personally, I do not see the practicality of employing a broadsword half the length of my body, but if I was in the woods, desert, or jungle, I would certainly avail myself to some of the better quality tactical tomahawks out there. Even the terrorists fear being sliced and diced with a blade – a tomahawk simply places American tradition into the skull of a fanatical enemy.

Nevertheless, unless you foresee an clear and demanding need to rip out someone's windpipe or pierce their lungs and heart repeatedly – which *all* long, thin, and sharp instruments are capable of – I would concentrate on the utility aspects of owning an edged weapon. Meaning, of course, that your blade will find its most effective use out where food, clothing, and shelter remain far more valuable than dispensing with a villain who would be better dispatched with a heavy hitting bullet. Owning a knife or tactical tomahawk is basically no different than owning a firearm. It represents a tool and little more. In *your* hands, it might save an innocent life, but there are far better tools out there with which to practice the trade.

Handguns

The handgun is, by far, the most practical weapon

---

[110] For a large assortment of edged weapons, visit www.trueswords.com.
[111] Eugene Sockut, *Secrets of Street Survival – Israeli Style: Staying Alive in a Civilian War Zone* (Boulder: Paladin Press, 1995), 89-152.

available for personal defense within the United States or other urbanized environments. Handguns come in a nearly infinite variety of sizes and shapes, from the small .22 caliber derringer revolvers on up to Wildey's .475 magnum auto pistol on through Smith & Wesson's behemoth .500 S&W magnum hunting revolvers.

For convenience, I am going to make two rather straightforward assumptions at this point. First, you remain dead serious about combating terrorism and you are eventually going to let people know where you *actively* stand on the issue. Second, because of this, your personal safety may be more at risk than if you were some timid and shy pastor at a tiny community church. Therefore, I will dispense with making any recommendations or references to calibers that are not considered adequate "man stoppers".

Furthermore, because this book is a *mini-manual* – meaning that it is supposed to be small and easily read within the shortest available time – I will equally dispense with the range of "my gun" versus "your gun" debates that necessarily arise from situations such as this. Manufacturer suggestions will be kept to the very minimum and caliber recommendations kept even narrower. There remains a wealth of knowledge available via the Internet and your local gun shop where you can – and *should* – research your own preferences.

Let us begin now with caliber selection for it represents the easiest to discuss. Even within the context of hunting, our society remains predicated upon foregoing stopping power for convenience. We just do not think "big" even when what we are aiming at may be pretty damn *big*. Whatever living thing that we shoot at, we must:

1. Hit a vital spot;

2. Hit that vital spot with a bullet that will hold together;

3. Throw a large enough bullet at that vital spot in order to create a *reliable* wound channel through the target.[112]

Too many people, whether hunting man or beast, subscribe to less powerful weapons for fear of "getting kicked" by the recoil of the firearm, but end upon sending round after round into their prey in order to subdue their target.[113]This is not restricted to hunting either. The durable .45 ACP cartridge was developed within the early years of the 20th century because its predecessor – the .38 – could not stop deranged Moro tribesmen in the Philippines who were hopped up on drugs. The smaller bullets (diameters measured in inches or millimeters) simply could not drop the attackers fast enough and many U.S. soldier or marine had emptied their six-shot revolvers into the fanatics to no avail; the .38 caliber service revolver was just too ineffective on maniacal subjects, such as the ones that you might encounter during the 21st century.

Take a look at the following comparison.[114]

.223/5.56mm   6.8 SPC   9 mm   .38   .40 S&W   .45 ACP   .308/7.62mm

---

[112] Ray Ordorica, "Use a Big Rifle" in *Gun Digest 49th Annual Edition* (Northbrook, IL: DBI Books, 1995), 195.
[113] Ibid., 197.
[114] Gray represents rifle bullets, black represents handgun or pistol bullets.

Each figure represents the approximate bore diameter of the respective caliber (allowing for expansion into the barrel grooving during firing). Even a casual glance will inform you that "bigger is better" when it comes to throwing bullet weight down range at your intended target. Added to this, is the cartridge length that runs the gamut depending upon the manufacturer's specifications. For example, the 7.62mm Kalashnikov (AK-47) assault rifle round is 39mm in length, whereas the 7.62mm NATO round has a length of 51mm, and the 7.62mm rimmed round used in Russian long rifles possesses a length of 54mm.

Two bullets of the same caliber may provide exceedingly different trajectories and performance, depending upon whether the round is a "long gun" round used for rifle shooting at distance or an "intermediate round" employed within assault rifles used primarily for close quarter combat. Next, we have to consider bullet *weight*, measured in grains, such as my .308 Winchester bullets of 168gr or my .45 ACP pistol rounds in 230gr. If this does not sound confusing enough, there represents a range of bullet *types* running the gamut from hollow-points that expand upon hitting their target to incendiaries that burst into flames when striking solid objects on through frangible rounds that disintegrate when hitting the same target. The reader is encouraged to read research the numerous capabilities.[115]

At the risk of inviting argument, I will simply recommend .45 ACP for male shooters and 9mm for smaller shooters such as women. Yes, the U.S. military has shifted over to exclusive use of the 9mm, but I prefer to employ a round with a history of taking down large, aggressive attackers

---

[115] I *highly* recommend shopping at www.ammunitiontogo.com for a range of choices and fast, efficient service to your front door.

even if the bullet does not expand as designed (which is how 9mm hollow points have entered the fray of preferences). A malfunctioning .45 makes a bigger hole than a malfunctioning 9mm.

Now, as for actual handguns. Here, too, remains a range of choices with the best, perhaps, resting with Smith & Wesson, Beretta, Glock, Taurus , Sig, Heckler and Koch, etc. With the range of "special ops" or "tactical" pistols on the market, there appears to be a sound, combat-proved firearm for nearly anyone's budget. Smith & Wesson offers, perhaps the widest selection economically and the better Model 1911 variants in .45 can run close to $1,000.[116] If you desire to do a lot of practice and do not wish to bother your neighbors, then you might want to choose a 1911 variant, such as those made by Sig-Sauer, with a threaded barrel for those locations that permit sound suppressors.

Assault Rifles

With the expiration of the ridiculous "assault weapons" ban, Americans are now free to purchase firearms that are durable, adaptable, and reliable. For the budget conscious, there remains a host of Kalashnikov rifles available, including AKM/AKMS (basically the modernized version of the AK-47 in semi-auto format) and the smaller 5.45x39mm caliber AK-74 as well as a range of pistol versions.[117] These American-made and/or imported rifles are easy to maintain and use and vast quantities of ammunition are available for them through various retailers. While not as accurate at distances as the American AR style rifles, they remain sufficient for targets out to ~400 meters. Not to mention, they

---

[116] Check www.impactguns.com and www.galleryofguns.com.
[117] See, for instance, www.atlanticfirearms.com.

will be almost exclusively used by your Islamist and narco terrorist enemies. Therefore, at worst, you would be doing yourself a favor in understanding these firearms that have been notoriously vilified by the media.

For those with a bit more money to spend ($1000 to $3000+), there remains an entire industry of AR assault rifles in calibers ranging from the omnipresent 5.56mm on up through .50 Beowulf. My personal "urban rifle" remains a Ruger SR-556 in 6.8mm SPC. This round bears a bit more punch when shooting through, say, glass, than the easily splintered 5.56mm.

The beauty of the AR-15 variants remains their ability to accept accessories for the rifles with Picatinny rails on them. These include scopes, red dot optics, reflex sights, lasers, night vision scopes, flashlights, even grenade launchers if you possess enough money. Spend your first dollar researching the many options available and you may spend upwards of a year deciding on the best firearm for you.

Shotguns

A reliable .12 gauge shotgun loaded with 00 Buck remains the best home defense weapon available in my opinion. Just the sound of a pump being chocked in the darkness can terrify even the most hardcore intruder. A semi-auto shotgun can fling a virtual barrier of buckshot or slugs downrange without the need for an extra arm to rack a new round into the chamber.

As with all firearms, the availability of products evolves faster than any legitimate book can discuss and this remains no different with shotguns. Winchester, Remington, and Mossberg represent just a few of the choices available and the uniqueness of the variety of ammunition makes the quality shotgun perhaps the best all-around firearm in existence. One gun can fire buckshot, slugs, tear gas, rubber bullets, flares, and even beanbags and breaching rounds to break down door hinges.

Remington's model 870 has been the military and police favorite for years and their new *887 NitroMag Tactical* offers a great option for those who fight the elements as well as assailants. Mossberg offers the best shotguns, perhaps, for those seeking to spend a little less money. One product, in particular, the *JIC* (Just in Case) *II* represents a "take down" version of the reliable Mossberg 500. Instead of the sealable tube that the other *JIC* models come in, the *JIC II* rests within a zippered nylon case that can attach to backpacks. The stockless, pistol-gripped shotgun is definitely *not* for recreational shooting, but can come in handy should you find yourself on the trail or bugging out after disaster strikes.

The entire shotgun *can* be assembled in less than 1-2 minutes, but *practice* is advised as the procedure can escape one's attention rather quickly and, frankly, it serves little purpose to own the gun if you cannot assemble, load, and fire it before the threat reaches you. For most, I would recommend it as a gun that you will assemble once you reach your destination regardless of perceived threats.

Long Rifles

A long rifle for anything beyond hunting is probably not within your interests unless you cannot own handguns or purchase assault rifles where you live. A few diehards out there will probably seek to develop some form of personal sniper rifle and, well, go for it. For the uninitiated, a long rifle usually means that you are targeting beyond 300-400 meters and that means that you generally live outside the urban environment. For the rest of us mortals, there exists absolutely no reason to believe that we need high-powered, expensive rifles with even more expensive and powerful scopes for what amounts to "up close and personal" work dealing with urban terrorists.[118]

Much can be done with standard hunting rifles as well as various military surplus rifles, such as the WWII-era Russian Mosin-Nagant (chambered in 7.62x54R) or the 1950s Yugoslavian Mauser M-48 (firing an 8mm cartridge), both of which can be purchased in quantities in excellent shape for about $200 each. As these very words are being typed, the I-96 corridor in Southeastern Michigan – a few miles from here – has been hit at least 22 times by an unknown shooter engaging vehicular traffic.[119] From what I have seen of the damage to the cars, this appears to be a larger caliber firearm, despite the police suspecting a handgun of some sort. Just a lesson in that threats can materialize from anywhere and from anyone...

A suitable, though more expensive, modern rifle are the PTR 91 series of H&K-inspired rifles in calibers ranging from 7.62x39mm to 7.62 NATO. The "paratrooper" version, which I own, the PTR-91 KFM4 makes for a fine urban battle rifle packing punch in a reduced size and yet offer three Picatinny rails to support bipods, lights, etc.[120] It represents a sound and beautiful weapon to behold.

---

[118] John West, *Fry the Brain: The Art of Urban Sniping and its Role in Modern Guerrilla Warfare* (Countryside, VA: SSI, 2008), 20-22.
[119] See http://www.nydailynews.com/news/national/i-96-mystery-sniper-strikes-wounded-article-1.1194140, accessed October 29, 2012.
[120] Visit www.PTR91.com.

9 REALITY CHECK.

There remains no more gruesome prospect to behold than the killing and maiming of another human being. The mere thought of a high-power bullet tearing through human flesh is more than most can withstand, which is why I intentionally truncated the weapons section of this second, more distributed version of *Mini-Manual of the Independent Counterterrorist*. However, if you are going to prepare for all "possibilities", including, specifically, shooting another human individual, than you must fully understand the implications of your or another's actions. Simply put, *never* aim a firearm at another living soul *unless you intend to kill them* and bear the legal, moral, and psychological implications of your action. Think of this as your "***Point a gun, go to jail; Use a gun, go to prison for life***.." rule.

Wound Ballistics

The primary property of a modern bullet in flight remains its velocity and its stability is affected by the spin imparted upon it from the rifling within the firearm's barrel. In this environment, the bullet rests within its realm and will carry through on its trajectory towards the ground under the auspices of gravity *unless* it impacts upon a target.

When the bullet strikes human tissue – at roughly 800 to 900 times denser than air[121] – it immediately destabilizes and begins to tumble releasing its energy and causing injury in three ways (assuming that it did not represent a *powerful enough* bullet that would pass through the body). The first representing the cutting and crushing of tissue as the bullet initially tries to slice through the body. The second mechanism involves the shock wave produced by supersonic bullets; this travels outwards at the speed of sound within water – 4,800 feet per second.[122]

The third injury causing mechanism represents *temporary cavitation*. The bullet forces energy outward and *forward* when it enters the body, even producing momentum for long after the bullet has exited the victim. This energy release causes the formation of the large cavity that essentially consists of the wound track and may be upwards of *thirty times* the bullet diameter.[123] This effect remains so violent that it may destroy capillaries far removed from the actual path of the bullet.

Perhaps, it would behoove us to examine things from a different perspective. Let us take a less technical view of the 5.56mm round. At distances of less than 100 yards, it is traveling at nearly three thousand feet per second when it impacts against the human body. The bullet, being small and unstable now, begins to tumble at, perhaps, ninety degrees before it reaches a full four inches into the body and begins

---

[121] Adrian Gilbert, *Sniper: One on One: The World of Combat Sniping* (London: Sidgwick & Jackson, 1994), 124.
[122] Ibid., 125.
[123] Ibid., 126.

to disintegrate into small fragments.[124] What had just been traveling at greater than the speed of sound – as if a military jet fighter on full afterburner – *stops* in a matter of a few inches. All that momentum has to go *somewhere* and that somewhere represents the body's tissues, bones, and blood vessels.

What was once healthy living 'body' now remains a conduit for a supersonic shockwave traveling up virtually every blood vessel, through every cell, and reverberating within every fluid within your body. They literally explode until the energy is dissipated. I will spare you the rest, but just remember the slight "shock" of, say, your leg when it hits the ground a bit too hard. Imagine that shock amplified thousands of times.

The human body is *not* rigid like a mannequin. It is mostly fluid with relatively few bones to keep the fluids and soft tissue into shape. What one part of your body experiences, the others share to a degree (we learned this through cross-training). Therefore, a bullet hitting a human body (or animal body for that matter) does not simply "drill" a hole through a solid object. It *pierces* a fluid object and the resulting shock waves literally vaporize anything that is not solid. Should this "fluid object" represent, say, the human brain, then the resulting damage magnifies exponentially as untold millions of electrical impulses are delivered throughout the body *instantaneously*. Chickens are *not* the only animals that can scurry around without heads attached…

Shot in Self Defense

You have just been involved within a shooting at a mall,

---

[124] Ibid., 129.

what do you do? First *you* have to call the 911 operator and report the matter – *do not trust anyone else on this matter!* Tell the operator your full name and *complete description*. Tell him or her that you were shot at (or about to be shot at) and had to defend your life because you experienced a grave fear *and* that you possess a concealed carry permit. Describe the (hopefully) one shot to the utmost detail. Do *not* just say that some ugly ass white guy accosted your wife. Describe their clothing in detail (e.g., white sleeveless tee shirt, tan trousers, New York Yankees jacket, etc.) as well as your own. *Tell the operator that you will lay down your weapon and surrender to the police as soon as they arrive.*

When the police arrive, announce yourself as the shooter, place your gun down slowly and calmly upon the floor, remind them that you bear a concealed carry permit, and then do *exactly* as they tell you without adding any further comments. You will likely be escorted down to the station to make a statement and once there, go ahead and ask for a public defender. Do not use your personal attorney as he or she is probably miles away and the public defender will likely be right down the hall.

The local DA may not particularly like your self-preservation efforts, so long before you even come near to getting into such trouble, do not include hand reloads in your gun or else they may consider you as being "pre-meditated" for hand-loading your ammunition specifically "for the crime". And, lastly, if the mall people attempt to sue you for bringing a gun into their "gun-free" establishment, go ahead and counter-sue for not protecting your life in the first place. In short, however, expect to be treated by all as if a criminal and have your life disrupted for years – if not forever. At least you will *still* be alive.

Some Final Lessons

"*War is cruelty, and you cannot refine it.*"
Gen. William Tecumseh Sherman
"*In the end, we simply cut and ran. The American national will had collapsed...*"
Graham A. Martin, former U.S. Ambassador to South Vietnam"
"*One committed to dying can be slain.*"
Sun-tzu

Yours is going to become a very lonely life. It just cannot be helped. You will find yourself tucked up against a wall of resentment no matter where you go. On the one hand, you will have the terrorists and their sympathizers. Those you can probably deal with because they represent largely known qualities. On the other hand, however, you will find yourself confronted with people who will take exception to what you are doing. Amongst these are the *perennial complainers* ("It's all the government's fault"; "Blame the wealthy", etc.); the *confused* ("Listen, I work in a school and the police told *me* exactly what to do, therefore I know a thing or two about terrorism", etc.); and, of course, the *Anti-Religion/Wrong Religion* crowd ("I do not believe in all of these "High and Mighty' people, they are just a bunch of hypocrites!" or, conversely, "You're maligning the Muslims unfairly!").

You have dealt with these people all of your life. They represent the ones who will, for instance, drive a Ford pickup truck and inform you of every single Chevrolet they have seen broken down along the highway or vice versa. They represent the kind of people who *will not* vote simply because their particular candidate got bumped out during the primaries. Worse, still, are the ones who profoundly believe in Bigfoot, UFOs, and "professional" wrestling but will not admit to it being a form of religion on their part.

They will deny *your* opinion because they cannot believe how anyone could ignore *their* evidence. You might see a mangy bear scratching himself against a tree or a particularly bright manifestation of the planet Venus, but that does not appear to faze them because "it all represents a great big government cover-up". You cannot do anything with these people, so you will just end up ignoring them for the long haul.

Like I said, yours is going to represent a *very lonely* life. You will find yourself spending more and more time *researching* than *entertaining*. You will notice that when you read, you read military and historical texts. When you watch television, you are probably glued to *Fox News* or *The Military Channel*. When you receive your tax refund check, you are not thinking about getting new tires for your car or finally calling the plumber to fix that leaky sink, you are thinking about how much more ammo you can purchase so that you can practice just a little bit more.

They have always said that it remains lonely at the *top*, but you will be wading through the putrid bottom. Any spare time that you can extract from your "necessitates" will be worked into your already strained counterterrorism schedule. You have much research to do, many supplies to order, and technology to inquire about. While information technology may have never represented your forte – too many concentrate on securing the networks to the exclusion of taking the fight to the terrorists – you are still interested in setting up a grid computing network within your home.[125] You will want to turn all those PCs, tablets, and laptops within your home into a 'poor man's supercomputer' for analyzing threats and assimilating Geospatial Intelligence."

Yet, what makes you feel lonely is perhaps the knowledge that few people – even those who once purported to have understood the Global War on Terror – believe that the Islamists or the narco cartels remain as much a threat as you know them to be. You have come across some compatriots, but they just did not quite pan out. You found that they usually belonged to one of the foregoing groups of people. They, for instance, wanted to use their guns for mayhem or some other ridiculous task. You may have found yourself mumbling, "I am *not* forming some form of 'Redneck Army' here – I am a professional!" And you *are*.

Others from the "government knows best" crowd, who blindly venture through life believing that they are always protected will think ill of you. These represent the people who do not wear seatbelts because airbags will protect them from injury. Had they ever bothered to watch videos of crash test dummies having their heads thrown through the rear windows, they would understand that seatbelts are required *particularly* with airbags. Local bureaucrats who believe you to represent some form of innate threat to the observable universe remain far too numerous to reflect upon here.

This may appear to represent a very depressing way of life besides one that remains inherently lonely, but it really is not. I find immense joy and satisfaction, not to mention a strong sense of duty in what I do and for which I remain

---

[125] Ahmar Abbas, *Grid Computing: A Practical Guide to Technology and Applications* (Hingham, MA: Charles River Media, 2004), 32-41.

confident has attracted you to combating terrorism in your own little way too. There is a strong sense of pride (patriotic and otherwise) in knowing that you must keep on your toes every minute of every day for decades on end. That you must examine, too, every little facet of your life and habits.

While others continually purchase lottery tickets because "Sooner or later, I will be lucky!" you practice and prepare for survival because sooner or later, you will definitely *not* be so lucky. You simply cannot accept chances with your life. Your team loses because they failed to prepare, *not* because the referees were screwy or the weather was against them, or there were too many injuries. You expect bad things to happen and pray daily that God keeps them to a minimum – not expect good things and only pray to God when the truly horrible arrives. You use the tools that He gave to you to continue living because you understand that the "other guy" may be praying too and God generally does not play favorites.

Yes, your life will indeed become lonely, but very exciting – just like the astronomer of old who sat high up in his mountaintop observatory consciously observing the night sky. He did not seek fame or fortune. He did it simply to understand the sheer beauty and complexity of the world before him. He could see threats out there – threats that could, someday, extinguish the human race – but he also knew that he might not be around when they came into play. His work existed just so that humanity could survive from his efforts…

RECOMMEND READING

Abbas, A. (2004). *Grid Computing: A Practical Guide to Technology and Applications.* Hingham, MA: Charles River Media, Inc.

Akhavan, J. (2006). *The Chemistry of Explosives* (Second Edition ed.). Cambridge, England: Royal Society of Chemistry.

Allison, G. (2004). *Nuclear Terrorism: The Ultimate Preventable Catastrophe.* New York: Times Books.

al-Qaeda. (n.d.). Declaration of Jihad (Holy War) Against the Country's Tyrants, Military Series.

Argonne National Laboratory. (2005). *Radiological Disperal Device (RDD).* Chicago: Argonne National Laboratory.

Army, United States. (1969). *TM 31-210 Improvised Munitions Handbook.* Washington: Department of the Army.

Baer, R. (2010, April). *Politics: GQ.* Retrieved April 17, 2010, from GQ Magazine Web site: http://www.gq.com/news-politics/politics/201004/dagger-to-the-cia

Baer, R. (2002). *See No Evil: The True Story of a Ground Soldier in the CIA's War on Terrorism.* New York: Three Rivers Press.

Balor, P. (1988). *Manual of the Mercenary Soldier.* Boulder: Paladin Press.

Beevor, A. (1998). *Stalingrad: The Fateful Siege: 1942-1943.* New York: Penguin Books.

Belfield, R. (2005). *The Assassination Business: A history of state-sponsored murder.* New York: Carroll & Graf Publishers.

Bennett, M., Bradbury, J., DeVries, K., Dickie, I., & Jestice, P. (2005). *Fighting Techniques of the Medieval World.* New York: Thomas Dunne Books.

Benson, R. (1986). *Gunrunning for Fun & Profit.* Boulder: Paladin Press.

Biddle, S., & Friedman, J. A. (2008). *THE 2006 LEBANON CAMPAIGN AND THE FUTURE OF WARFARE: Implications for Army and Defense Policy.* Carlisle, PA: Strategic Studies Institute.

Black, I., & Morris, B. (1991). *Israel's Secret Wars: A History of Israel's Intelligence Services.* New York: Grove Press.

Blandford, E. L. (2000). *SS Intelligence.* Shrewsbury, England: Airlife Publishing Ltd.

Bledowska, C., & Bloch, J. (1987). *KGB/CIA Intelligence and Counter-Intelligence Operations.* London: Bison Books.

Bodansky, Y. (2007). *Chechen Jihad: Al-Qaeda's Training Ground and the Next Wave of Terror.* New York: Harper.

Bodansky, Y. (1994). *TERROR! The inside story of the terrorist conspiracy in America.* SPI Books.

Bowden, M. (2001). *Killing Pablo: The Hunt for the World's Greatest Outlaw.* New York: Penguin Books.

Brands, H. (2010). *Crime, Violence, and the Crisis in Guatemala: A Case Study in the Erosion of the State.* Carlisle: Strategic Studies Institute.

Brands, H. (2009). *Dealing with Political Ferment in Latin America: the Populist Revival, the Emergence of the Center, and Implication for U.S. Policy.* Carlisle, PA: Strategic Studies Institute.

Brands, H. (2009). *Mexico's Narco-Insurgency and U.S. Counterdrug Policy.* Carlisle, PA: Strategic Studies Institute.

Bullock, A. (1993). *Hitler and Stalin: Parallel Lives.* New York: Vintage.

Byman, D. (2005). *Deadly Connections: States that Sponsor Terrorism.* New York: Cambridge University Press.

Celeski, J. D. (2010). *Hunter-Killer Teams: Attacking Enemy Safe Havens.* Hurlburt Field: Joint Special Operations University.

Chinnery, P. D. (1994). *Any Time, Any Place: A history of USAF air commando and special operations forces.* Annapolis: Naval Institue Press.

Clark, R. M. (2007). *Intelligence Analysis: A target-centric approach.* Washington: CQ Press.

Clausewitz, C. v. (1984). *On War.* (M. H. Paret, Trans.) Princeton: Princeton University Press.

Coll, S. (2004). *Ghost Wars: The Secret History of the CIA, Afghanistan, and Bin Laden, from the Soviet Invasion to Steptember 10, 2001.* New York: Penguin Books.

Colling, R. L., & York, T. W. (2010). *Hospital and Healtchare Security* (5th Edition ed.). Burlington, MA: Elsevier.

Cox, R. (1983). Total Terrorism: Argentina, 1969 to 1979. In M. Crenshaw, *Terrorism, Legitimacy, and Power* (pp. 124-142). Middletown, CT: Wesleyan.

Crawford, S. (1997). *Deadly Fighting Skills of the World.* London: Brown Books.

Dashti, A. (1994). *Twenty Three Years: A study of the Prophetic Career of Mohammad.*

Dauber, C. I. (2009). *YouTube War: Fighting in a World of Cameras in every Cell Phone and Photoshop on every Computer.* Carlisle, PA: Strategic Studies Institute.

DeFronzo, J. (2011). *Revolutions and Revolutionary Movements* (Fourth ed.). Boulder, CO: Westview Press.

Department of the Army. (2005). *FM 3-05.30 PSYCHOLOGICAL OPERATIONS.* Washington: United States Government.

Dewar, M. (1992). *War in the Streets: The Story of Urban Combat from Calais to Khafji.* London: David & Charles.

Dobson, C., & Payne, R. (1982). *Counterattack: The West's battle against the terrorists.* New York: Facts on File, Inc.

Dunigan, M., Hoffman, D., Chalk, P., Nichiporuk, B., & Deluca, P. (2012). *Characterizing and Exploring the Implications of Maritime Irregular Warfare.* Santa Monica, CA: RAND Corporation.

Durant, W. (1950). *The Age of Faith.* New York: Simon and Schuster.

Ehrenfeld, R. (2003). *Funding Evil: How Terrorism is Financed -- and How to Stop it.* Chicago: Bonus Books.

Ellis, J. W. (2007). *Police Analysis and Planning for Homicide Bombings: Prevention, Defense, and Response.* Springfield, IL: Charles C. Thomas Publisher, Ltd.

Ellis, R. E. (2011). *China-Latin America Military Engagement: Good Will, Good Business, and Strategic Position.* Carlisle, PA: Strategic Studies Institute.

Emerson, S. (2002). *American Jihad: The Terrorists Living Amongst Us.* New York: The Free Press.

England, J. W. (1987). *Long-Range Patrol Operations: Reconnaissance, Combat, and Special Operations.* Boulder: Paladin Press.

Fishel, J. T., & Manwaring, M. G. (2006). *Uncomfortable Wars Revisited.* Norman, OK: University of Oklahoma Press.

Fowler, W. (2005). *The Special Forces Guide to Escape and Evasion.* New York: Thomas Dunne Books.

Frey, B. S. (2007). *Why Kill Politicians? A Rational Choice Analysis of Political Assassinations.* Basel: Center for Research in Economics, Management and the Arts.

Gabriel, M. A. (2006). *Journey into the Mind of an Islamic Terrorist.* Lake Mary, Florida: Front Line.

Gander, T. (1990). *Guerrilla Warfare Weapons: The Modern Underground Fighter's Armoury.* New York: Sterling Publishing Co.,

Inc.

Gerges, F. (2006). *Journey of the Jihadist: Inside Muslim Militancy.* Orlando: Harcourt.

Gilbert, A. (1994). *Sniper: One on One: The World of Combat Sniping.* London: Sidgwick & Jackson.

Glasstone, S., & Dolan, P. J. (1977). *The Effects of Nuclear Weapons* (Third Edition ed.). Washington: United States Department of Defense; United States Department of Energy.

Glazebrook, J., & Nicholson, N. (2003). *Executive Protection Specialist Handbook* (Second Edition ed.). Shawnee Mission, Kansas: Varro Press.

Godlewski, R. (2008). Cultivating Creativity within Intelligence Analysis. *American Intelligence Journal , 25* (2), 85-87.

Godlewski, R. (2011). Financial Counterintelligence: Fractioning the Lifeblood of Asymmetrical Warfare. *American Intelligence Journal , 29* (2), 24-33.

Godlewski, R. (2009). Human Intelligence: Perceiving an Enemy's Thoughts. *American Intelligence Journal , 27* (1), 29-37.

Godlewski, R. (2006). *Integrated Technical Warfare: An Organizational Guide to Creating a Corporate Counterterrorism Force.* Michigan: Road Sailor Books.

Godlewski, R. (2011). Latte Intelligence: The Divorce of Shock Creativity and Special Information Operations. *American Intelligence Journal , 29* (1), 70-79.

Godson, R. (2008). *Dirty Tricks or Trump Cards: U.S. Cover Action & Counterintelligence.* New Brunsick (U.S.A.): Transaction Publishers.

Goodman, M. (2007). *Rome and Jerusalem: The Clash of Ancient Civilizations.* New York: Alfred A. Knopf.

Goodrich, T. (1997). *Scalp Dance: Indian Warfare on the High Plains 1865-1879.* Mechanicsburg , Pennsylvania: Stackpole Books.

Gourevitch, P. (1998). *We wish to inform you that tomorrow we will be killed with our families.* New York: Picador.

Gray, C. S. (2006). *Another Bloody Century: Future Warfare.* London: Phoenix.

Grayson, G. W. (2010). *La Familia Drug Cartel: Implications for U.S.-Mexican Security.* Carlisle, PA: Strategic Studies Institute.

Grayson, G. W. (2011). *Threat Posed by Mounting Vigilantism in Mexico.* Carlisle, PA: Strategic Studies Institute.

Gross, M. L. (2010). *Moral Dilemmas of Modern War: Torture, Assassination, and Blackmail in an Age of Asymmetric Conflict.* New York: Cambridge University Press.

Grossman, D. (2009). *On Killing: The Psychological Cost of Learning to Kill in War and Society* (Revised ed.). New York: Back Bay Books.

Guevara, E. (2007). *Guerrilla Warfare.* BN Publishing.

Harclerode, P. (2001). *Fighting Dirty: The Inside Story of Covert Operations from Ho Chi Minh to Osama Bin Laden.* London: Cassell & Company.

Harclerode, P. (2000). *Secret Soldiers: Special Forces in the War Against Terrorism.* London: Cassell & Company.

Harold A. Winters with Gerald E. Galloway, J. W. (1998). *Battling the Elements: Weather and terrain in the conduct of war.* Baltimore: Johns Hopkins University Press.

Hart, B. K. (1926). *Scipio Africanus: Greater than Napoleon.* Cambridge: Da Capo Press.

Hayes, S. K. (1981). *The Ninja and their secret fighting art.* Rutland, VT: Charles E. Tuttle Company.

Headquarters, Department of the Army. (2002). *FM 3-06 Combined Arms Operations in Urban Terrain.* Washington: Department of the Army.

Heiden, K. (1944). *Der Fuehrer: Hitler's rise to power.* Boston: Houghton Mifflin Company.

Herzog, C. (1982). *The Arab-Israeli Wars: War and Peace in the Middle East from the War of Independence through Lebanon.* New York: Vintage.

Heuer Jr., R. J., & Pherson, R. H. (2011). *Structured Analytic Techniques For Intelligence Analysis.* Washington: CQ Press.

Hoffman, B. (2006). A Nasty Business. In R. D. Howard, & R. L. Sawyer, *Terrorism and Counterterrorism: Understanding the New Security Environment: Readings and Interpretations* (pp. 402-407). Dubuque, Iowa: McGraw-Hill.

Hoffman, F. G. (2007, April). Mind Maneuvers: The Psychological Element of Counterinsurgency Warfare can be the Most Persuasive. *Armed Forces Journal* , pp. 28-32.

Holder, P. T., & Hawley, D. L. (1998). *The Executive Protection Professional's Manual.* Boston: Butterworth-Heinemann.

Hourani, A. (1991). *A History of the Arab Peoples.* New York: Warner Books.

Hristov, J. (2010). Self-Defense Forces, Warlords, or Criminal Gangs? Towards a New Conceptualization of Paramilitarism in Colombia. *Labour, Capital & Society* , *43* (2), 14-56.

Joes, A. J. (2007). *Urban Guerrilla Warfare.* Lexington: University Press of Kentucky.

Johnson, W. R. (2009). *Thwarting Enemies at Home and Abroad: How to be a Counterintelligence Officer.* Washington: Georgetown University Press.

Jomini, A.-H. (2007). *The Art of War.* (G. Mendell, & W. Craighill, Trans.) Rockville, MD: Arc Manor.

Jones, A., Kovacich, G. I., & Luzwick, P. G. (2002). *Global Information Warfare: How Businesses, Governments, and Others Achieve Objectives and Attain Competitive Advantages.* New York: Auerbach.

Jones, I. (2010). *The Human Factor: Inside the CIA's Dysfunctional Intelligence Culture.* New York: Encounter Books.

Kagan, D. (2003). *The Peloponnesian War.* New York: Viking.

Kahaner, L. (2007). *AK-47: The weapon that changed the face of war.* Hoboken: John Wiley & Sons, Inc.

Kan, P. R. (2008). *Drug Intoxicated Irregular Fighters: Complications, Dangers, and Responses.* Carlisle, PA: Strategic Studies Institute.

Kan, P. R. (2011). *Mexico's "Narco-Refugees": The Looming Challenge for U.S. National Security.* Carlisle, PA: Strategic Studies Institute.

Karp, A. (1996). *Ballistic Missile Proliferation: The Politics and Technics.* New York: SIPRI/Oxford University Press.

Kellner, T., & Pipitone, F. (2010). Inside Mexico's Drug War. *World Policy Journal* , 29-37.

Kelly, J. (2004). *Gunpowder: Alchemy, Bombards, & Pyrotechnics: The History of the Explosive that Changed the World.* New York: Basic Books.

Knott, S. F. (1996). *Secret and Sanctioned: Covert operations and the American presidency.* New York: Oxford University Press.

Koch, O. W. (1999). *G-2: Intelligence for Patton.* Atglen: Schiffer Military History.

Kokoski, R. (1995). *Technology and the Proliferation of Nuclear Weapons.* New York City: sipri/Oxford University Press.

Kouzminov, A. (2005). *Biological Espionage: Special Operations of the Soviet and Russian Foreign Intelligence Services in the West.* London: Greenhill Books.

Kreeft, P. (1990). *Everything you ever wanted to know about Heaven but never dreamed of asking!* San Francisco: Ignatius.

Krepinevich, A. F. (2010). *7 Deadly Scenarios: A Military Futurist Explores War in the Twenty-First Century.* New York: Bantam Books.

Kybett, H., & Boysen, E. (2008). *All New Electronics Self-Teaching Guide* (Third Edition ed.). Indianapolis: Wiley Publishing, Inc.

Lance, P. (2003). *1000 years for revenge: International terrorism and the FBI -- the untold story.* New York: Regan Books.

Laqueur, W. (1987). *The Age of Terrorism.* Boston: Little, Brown and Company.

Lawrence, T. (1935). *Seven Pillars of Wisdom.* New York: Doubleday, Doran & Company, Inc.

Lee, G. D. (2004). *Global Drug Enforcement: Practical Investigative Techniques.* Boca Raton, FL: CRC Press.

Leebaert, D. (2006). *To Dare and to Conquer: Special Operations and the Destiny of Nations from Achilles to Al Qaeda.* New York: Back Bay Books.

Lung, H. (1997). *Assassin! The Deadly Art of the Cult of the Assassins.* New York: Citadel Press.

Lung, H. (2006). *Mind Control: The Ancient Art of Psychological Warfare.* New York: Citadel Press.

Machiavelli, N. (1903). *The Prince.* (L. Ricci, Trans.) London: Grant Richards.

Manwaring, M. G. (2009). *A "New" Dynamic in the Western Hemisphere Security Environment: The Mexican Zetas and Other Private Armies.* Carlisle: Strategic Studies Institute.

Manwaring, M. G. (2009). *State and Nonstate Associated Gangs: Credible "Midwives of New Social Orders".* Carlisle: Strategic Studies Institute.

Marcella, G. (2008). *War without Borders: The Colombia-Ecuador Crisis of 2008.* Carlisle, PA: Strategic Studies Institute.

Marighella, C. *Mini-Manual of the Urban Guerrilla.*

Martines, L. (2012). Mexican Crime Cartels. *Journal of Counterterrorism & Homeland Security International , 18* (1), 36-40.

May, T. (2007). *THE MONGOL ART OF WAR: Chinggis Khan and the Mongol Military System* (Book Club ed.). Yardley, PA: Westholme Publishing.

McRaven, W. H. (1996). *SPEC OPS: Case Studies in Special Operations Warfare: Theory and Practice.* New York: Ballantine Books.

Melton, H. K., & Wallace, R. (2009). *The Official C.I.A. Manual of Trickery and Deception.* New York: William Morrow.

Morris, B. (1997). *Israel's Border Wars 1949-1956.* New York: Oxford University Press, Inc.

Oatman, R. L. (2006). *Executive Protection: New Solutions for a New Era.* Arnold, Maryland: Noble House.

Paladin Press. (1991). *Federal Bomb Intelligence: U.S. Government Guide to Terrorist Explosives.* Boulder: Paladin Press.

Paladin Press. (1993). *KGB Alpha Team Training Manual: How the Soviets Trained for Personal Combat, Assassination, and Subversion.* Boulder: Paladin Press.

Peters, R. (2006, December). Killing with Kindness: Political correctness infiltrates the Army. *Armed Forces Journal* , pp. 28-32.

Peters, R. (2007, January). Rebels and Religion: How fighters become fanatics. *Armed Forces Journal* , pp. 28-31.

Peters, R. (2007, September). When Muslim armies won: Lessons from yesteryears's jihadi victories. *Armed Forces Journal* , pp. 38-41,47.

Poole, H. J. (2007). *Dragon Days: Time for "Unconventional" Tactics.* Emerald Isle, NC: Posterity Press.

Poole, H. J. (2005). *Militant Tricks: Battlefield Ruses of the Islamic Insurgent.* Emerald Isle, North Carolina: Posterity Press.

Poole, H. J. (2004). *Tactics of the Crescent Moon: Militant Muslim Combat Methods.* Emerald Isle, North Carolina: Posterity Press.

Rabinovich, A. (2004). *The Yom Kippur War: The Epic Encounter that Transformed the Middle East.* New York: Schocken.

Randal, J. (2004). *Osama: The Making of a Terrorist.* New York: Vintage Books.

Rassler, D., & Brown, V. (2011). *The Haqqani Nexis and the Evolution of al-Qa'ida.* United States Military Academy. West Point: The Combating Terrorism Center at West Point.

Reisman, W. M., & Antoniou, C. T. (1994). *The Laws of War: A comprehensive collection of primary documents on international laws governing armed conflict.* New York: Random House.

Richelson, J. T. (2008). *The U.S. Intelligence Community* (Fifth Edition ed.). Boulder: Westview Press.

The Seven Military Classics of Ancient China. (1993). (R. D. Sawyer, Trans.) Boulder: Westview Press.

Schroen, G. C. (2007). *First In: An Isider's Account of How the CIA Spearheaded the War on Terror in Afghanistan.* New York: Ballantine Books.

Schweitzer, D. (2002). *Securing the Network from Malicious Code: A Complete Guide to Defending Against Viruses, Worms, and Trojans.* Indianapolis: Wiley Publishing, Inc.

Shulsky, A. N., & Schmitt, G. J. (2002). *Silent Warfare: Understanding the World of Intelligence* (Third Edition ed.). Washington: Potomac Books.

Shultz Jr., R. H. (2006). Showstoppers: Nine Reasons Why We Never Sent Our Special Operations Forces after al Qaeda before 9/11. In R. D. Howard, *Terrorism and Counterterrorism: Understanding the New Security Environment: Readings and Interpretations* (Second Edition ed., pp. 518-530). Dubuque, IA: McGraw-Hill.

Simpson, C. (1994). *Science of Coercion: Communications Research & Psychological Warfare 1945-1960.* New York: Oxford University Press.

Sockut, E. (1995). *Secrets of Street Survival -- Israeli Style: Staying alive in a Civilian War Zone.* Boulder: Paladin Press.

Spencer, R. (2006). *The Truth about Muhammad: Founder of the World's Most Intolerant Religion.* Washington: Regnery Publishing.

Sperry, P. (2005). *Infiltration: How Muslim Spies and Subversives have*

Penetrated Washington. Nashville: Nelson Current.

Spicer, M. (2011). Mexican Drug Cartels: The Growing Threat of the Sniper Attack. *Journal of Counterterrorism & Homeland Security International , 16* (4), 48-50.

Sprinzak, E. (1998). The psychopolitical formation of extreme left terrorism in a democracy: The case of the Weathermen. In W. Reich, *Origins of Terrorism: Psychologies, Ideologies, Theologies, States of Mind* (pp. 65-85). Washington: Woodrow Wilson Center Press.

Steele, R. D. (2010). *Human Intelligence: All Humans, All Minds, All the Time.* Carlisle, PA: Strategic Studies Institute.

Stoll, C. (1990). *The Cuckoo's Egg: Tracking a spy through the maze of computer espionage.* New York: Pocket Books.

Summers Jr, H. G. (1982). *On Strategy: A Critical Analysis of the Vietnam War.* New York: Presidio Press.

Swanson, S. (2007, May). Viral Targeting of the IED Social Network System. *Small Wars Journal ,* pp. 2-16.

Taber, R. (2002). *War of the Flea: The Classic Study of Guerrilla Warfare.* Washington: Potomac Books.

Terrill, W. A. (2011). *The Saudi-Iranian Rivalry and the Future of Middle East Security.* Carlisle, PA: Strategic Studies Institute.

Thomas, E. (2006). *The Very Best Men: The Daring Early Years of the CIA.* New York: Simon & Schuster.

Thomas, H. (1993). *Conquest: Montezuma, Cortes, and the Fall of Old Mexico.* New York: Simon and Schuster.

Thomas, T. L. (2005). Russian Tactical Lessons Learned Fighting Chechen Separatists. *Journal of Slavic Military Studies , 18,* pp. 731-766.

Thornton, R. (2011). *Organizational Change in the Russian Airborne Forces: The Lessons of the Georgian Conflict.* Carlisle, PA: Strategic Studies Institute.

Tierney, J. (2012, March). Know Thy Enemy's Weapons: The Army Needs to Step Up Training on Foreign Arms. *Armed Forces Journal* , 8-10,30.

Timmerman, K. R. (2006). *Countdown to Crisis: The Coming Nuclear Showdown with Iran.* New York: Three Rivers Press.

Tomajczyk, S. F. (1999). *Bomb Squads.* Osceola, WI: MBI Publishing.

Toolis, K. (1995). *Rebel Hearts: Journeys Within the IRA's Soul.* New York: St. Martin's Griffin.

Truesdell, M. (1997). *Spectacular Politics: Louis-Napoleon Bonaparte and the Fete Imperiale, 1849-1870.* New York City: Oxford University Press.

Tucker, D. (1998, Summer). Fighting Barbarians. *Parameters* , pp. 69-79.

Tucker, J. B. (2006). *War of Nerves: Chemical Warfare from World War I to Al-Qaeda.* New York: Pantheon.

United States Army. (2005). *FMI 3-34.119 Improvised Explosive Device Defeat.* Fort Leonard Wood: Department of the Army.

United States Catholic Conference, Inc. (1994). *Catechism of the Catholic Church.* New York: Doubleday.

United States Department of the Army. (1961). *FM 31-21 Guerrilla Warfare and Special Forces Operations.* Washington: U.S. War Office.

United States Marine Corps. (1987). *MCDP 2 Intelligence.* Washington: United States Government.

Utley, R. L. (1989, Autumn). Crook and Miles, Fighting and Feuding on the Indian Frontier. *MHQ: The Quarterly Journal of Military History* , pp. 81-91.

Vacca, J. R. (2002). *Computer Forensics: Computer Crime Scene Investigation.* Hingham, MA: Charles River Media, Inc.

Venter, A. J. (2007). *Allah's Bomb: The Islamic Quest for Nuclear Weapons.* Guilford, CT: The Lyons Press.

Waisberg, T. (2009). The Colombia-Ecuador Armed Crisis of March 2008: The Practice of Targeted Killing and Incursions against Non-State Actors Harbored at Terrorist Safe Havens in a Third Party State. *Studies in Conflict & Terrorism , 32*, 476-488.

Waller, D. C. (1994). *The Commandos: The inside story of America's secret soldiers.* New York: Simon & Schuster.

Walton, T. R. (1994). *The Spanish Treasure Fleets.* Sarasota: Pineapple Press.

Watkins, L. J. (2011). *Self-propelled Semi-submersibles: The Next Great Threat to Regional Security and Stability.* Monterey: Naval Post-Graduate School.

Waugh, B., & Keown, T. (2004). *Hunting the Jackal.* New York: Avon Books.

West, J. (2008). *Fry the Brain: The Art of Urban Sniping and its Role in Modern Guerrilla Warfare.* Countryside, VA: SSI.

Wilkinson, P. (1986). *Terrorism & the Liberal State* (Second Edition ed.). New York: New York University Press.

Williams, P. (2009). *Criminals, Militias, and Insurgents: Organized Crime in Iraq.* Carlisle, PA: Strategic Studies Institute.

Wilson, D. (2006). *Charlemagne.* New York: Doubleday.

Winters, H. A., Galloway Jr., G. E., Reynolds, W. J., & Rhyne, D. W. (1998). *Battling the Elements: Weather and terrain in the conduct of war.* Baltimore: Johns Hopkins University Press.

Zuhur, S. (2008). *HAMAS and ISRAEL: Conflicting Strategies of Group-Based Politics.* Carlisle, PA: Strategic Studies Institute.

ABOUT THE AUTHOR

R.J. Godlewski (GOD LESS KEY) is an independent counterterrorism consultant, the director of the private International Nuclear Emergency Response Team [INERT], and the author of several novels, commentaries, and professional articles. He is the author and architect of the Web-based *Independent Counterterrorist* training program. He is currently a graduate student at American Military University completing his M.A. in Military Studies, Asymmetrical Warfare concentration, and graduate certificate in Security Management. Mr. Godlewski holds a B.A. in Intelligence Studies, Terrorism Studies concentration with a minor degree in Area Studies – Middle East with honors from American Military University. He further holds an undergraduate certificate in Explosive Ordnance Disposal and is a veteran of both the United States Navy and Navy Reserve. His most recent article is "Financial Counterintelligence: Fractioning the Lifeblood of Asymmetrical Warfare" in *American Intelligence Journal* 29 no. 2 (2011): 24-33.

www.ingramcontent.com/pod-product-compliance
Lightning Source LLC
Chambersburg PA
CBHW070035300526
45794CB00001B/495